What YOUR CHILD NEEDS to KNOW About GOD

RON RHODES

HARVEST HOUSE PUBLISHERS
Eugene, Oregon 97402

WHAT YOUR CHILD NEEDS TO KNOW ABOUT GOD
Copyright © 1997 by Ron Rhodes
Published by Harvest House Publishers
Eugene, Oregon 97402

Library of Congress Cataloging-in-Publication Data

Rhodes, Ron
  What your child needs to know about God / Ron Rhodes
    p. cm.
  Includes biographical references.
  ISBN 1-56507-556-0
  1. Christian education—Home training. 2. Children—Religious life. 3. Children—Conversion to Christianity. I. Title.
  BV1590.R48 1997
  248.8'45—dc20   96–44912
                                                                        CIP

96   97   98   99   00   01   02   / BF /   10   9   8   7   6   5   4   3   2   1

To my wife Kerri

*"He who finds a wife finds what is good
and receives favor from the LORD."*

—Proverbs 18:22

Contents

Acknowledgments

There are three alone who deserve special mention here—the three who have taught me the most about parenthood: my beloved wife Kerri and my precious children, David and Kylie. You're the greatest!

Charlie Brown Says . . .

In a "Peanuts" comic strip, there was a conversation between Lucy and Charlie Brown. Lucy said that life is like a deck chair: Some people place it so they can see where they are going, some place it so they can see where they have been, and some place it so they can see where they are at present.

Charlie Brown replied, "I can't even get mine unfolded."

That's the way many Christian parents feel in their attempt to raise Christian children in a non-Christian world. No doubt about it—Christian parenting can be a challenge!

Not long ago I heard about a six-year-old boy named Arne who one day stomped his foot and firmly declared to his parents, "We're the only family that has to have goodness!"[1] Yes, Christian parenting can be a challenge!

I read about another Christian parent who, like many of us, had a particularly difficult day with her child. She reflects:

> My youngest son, Landon, and I frequently find our wills clashing. At the end of one particularly arduous day, when he was five years old, I found a note on my pillow that he had written with his limited spelling ability: "Dear Mommy, I luv you. I am sorry I wuz bad. From now on I will tri my best to be god."[2]

Christian parenting can be a challenge! (Landon, of course, meant to say "good.")

This book is all about what your child needs to know about God. Teaching our kids this is one of the most serious responsibilities we have as parents. We cannot afford to fail because we live in a world that is not sympathetic to Christianity or to Christian values.

Howard Hendricks, one of my professors at Dallas Theological Seminary, once said, "We are surrounded by foreign, hostile, and home-shattering influences in our world today. The supportive elements of society no longer feed and shade us. The Christian home must blossom in a field of weeds."[3] I think Dr. Hendricks is right.

In teaching his students how to become effective Christian parents, Dr. Hendricks went on to say that we have to learn to navigate in the midst of a storm. This is not the ideal—it's much better to learn to navigate in calm seas. But that's no longer an option for us. Our society is an ever-worsening sea of turbulence, so learn to navigate *we must*! Otherwise, *our children (along with us) sink*!

How to Use This Book

What Your Child Needs to Know About God was written to help you sail today's turbulent seas. My prayer as you read is that you will discover and rediscover lasting principles from Scripture that will enable you to effectively equip your kids for what lies ahead of them.

In the early chapters, we will build a foundation. We'll focus attention on such issues as teaching, training, and modeling for our children. Then, after laying this foundation, the rest of the book will focus specifically on the things your child needs to know about God.

In terms of how each chapter is structured, I need to tell you that part of each chapter is written *strictly for you* (the parent), and part of it is written with a view to helping you communicate the main points to your children. In my experience, I have found that not every parent feels they are well-versed enough in every doctrine to explain them fully to their children. So, with this in mind, in each chapter I have provided a mini-course on each doctrine for your benefit.

When going over this material with your children, don't attempt to cover an entire chapter in one sitting. That won't work. Teach them the things of God in bite-size nuggets. You will notice that each chapter can be divided into small sections. I recommend that you focus on a single section each time you teach your children. This makes it much more palatable for them.

Let me emphasize that these chapters focus on *the basics*. These chapters are engineered to help you teach your children the fundamentals of each of the doctrines covered. Because the chapters are not exhaustive, as your children grow older you will want to supplement with other, more detailed materials—especially on critically important issues such as drinking and drugs, premarital sex, the New Age infiltration of public schools, and the like.

Now, as a father I have certainly made my share of mistakes that have caused some regret for both me and my kids (this is confession time). I don't stand before you as the perfect parent. My goal as a perpetually learning parent is to share with you what I've learned from the best child-training manual there is—the Bible.

Toward that end, throughout most chapters in this book you will find "Pass It On" principles. In Scripture, living the Christian life is often compared to running a relay race (Acts 20:24; Galatians 5:7; 2 Timothy 4:7). After the first runner runs a lap, he passes a baton to the second runner, who then continues on in the race.

In this book, I compare the teaching and training of our children to passing a baton to them in a relay race. Passing the baton represents passing them the biblical principles they need in order to live a successful Christian life. Meditate upon these principles. Commit them to memory. Make them part of the fabric of your life.

You will also find in most chapters one or more "Sharing Time" ideas. These stories, word pictures, and illustrations will help you communicate a particular principle to your

children. You will find that teaching your children using illustrations can be very fun!

Through it all, my prayer is that you, like me, will learn
the truth of Psalm 127:1: "Unless the LORD builds the house,
its builders labor in vain."

Teach Your Children Well

1

Evangelizing Your Children

> "If Christendom is to be helped, one must
> begin with the children."[1]
>
> —*Martin Luther*

Evangelist Billy Graham is right when he says that "conversion is so simple that the smallest child can be converted."[2] The great Charles Spurgeon likewise said, "Children need to be saved and *may* be saved."[3] The apostle Paul, speaking to young Timothy, said, "*From infancy* you have known the holy Scriptures, which are able to make you wise for salvation through faith in Christ Jesus" (2 Timothy 3:15, emphasis added).

Obviously, if Timothy had been taught the Scriptures from infancy, it's never to early to begin sharing important gospel truths with our children. Timothy's mother started Timothy's training in the Scriptures at a very early age and continued this training throughout his childhood. I say this because of the present tense verb in this verse. The present tense indicates continuous, ongoing action. Timothy's mother didn't just sporadically talk to Timothy about the Scriptures; she regularly spoke to him about the Scriptures.

There are many people I can think of who have followed Timothy's lead in becoming Christians at a very young age. Corrie ten Boom was saved at age five, revivalist Jonathan Edwards at age seven, Billy Graham at age six, and his wife, Ruth, at age four.[4]

The condition of salvation is simple faith in Christ. It is a fact that the most trusting people in the world are children. Children have not acquired the obstructions to faith that often come with education. No wonder, then, that the Scriptures instruct us to become like children in order to enter into the kingdom of God (Matthew 18:3). As adults, we must develop the same kind of trust that little children naturally have.

Eric Stuyck, an expert in child evangelism, makes a keen observation for us from Matthew 18:1, where Jesus was asked by the disciples: "Who is the greatest in the kingdom of heaven?" Jesus answered by pointing to the model of a little child. It would be truly ridiculous to hold up a child as a model for someone entering the kingdom of heaven and hold at the same time that the little child is too young to become a part of that kingdom by placing faith in Christ.[5] In this same story, Jesus specifically referred to "these little ones who *believe* in me" (verse 6, emphasis added). Clearly, little children have the capacity to believe in Jesus.

Six Keys to Evangelizing Your Child

There is no set formula for evangelizing your child. But the following six points may be helpful to you. (You will find much more detailed help on sin, salvation, Jesus Christ, and God in the section "No Compromise.")

1. *Read Bible stories to your child that illustrate being lost and getting saved.* Children love to hear stories. Two of my favorite Bible stories that illustrate this truth are the parable of the lost sheep (Luke 15:4-7) and the parable of the lost coin (Luke 15:8-10).

2. *Use stories to explain humanity's sin problem.* I like to illustrate the sin problem by talking about a bow and arrow. If you aim at a target with a bow and arrow, sometimes you miss. This is one of the meanings of the word "sin" in the New Testament. In our lives we miss the target when we don't live as God wants us to. How do we know if our lives

are missing the mark? By measuring our lives against God's book—the Bible. God has told us what He wants us to do and what He doesn't want us to do. When we fail in these things, we've missed the target (Romans 5:12).

3. *Explain what Jesus accomplished at the cross.* God loves us very much. But because each of us has missed the target in our lives, there is a wall or barrier between us and God. Our relationship with God has been broken. Jesus, by dying on the cross, took the punishment for our sins so we wouldn't have to. He took it for us. Jesus made it possible for us to have our relationship to God restored.

I like to talk about the "certificate of debt" mentioned in Colossians 2:14 (NASB) as a means of illustrating this. (You might call it a "bad behavior list" when speaking to your child.) Back in ancient days, whenever someone was found guilty of a crime, he or she was put in jail and a bad behavior list was posted on the jail door. This paper listed all the crimes the offender was found guilty of. Upon release, after serving the prescribed time in jail, the offender was given the bad behavior list. It was stamped "Paid in Full."

Christ took the bad behavior list for each one of us and nailed it to the cross. He paid for *all* our sins at the cross. Jesus' sacrifice "paid in full" the price for our sins (John 19:30). Because of Jesus, the bad behavior list for each one of our lives has been tossed into the trash can. Our relationship with God is restored.

4. *Explain that salvation is a free gift that is received by faith in Jesus.* Ephesians 2:8,9 says salvation is a gift from God. A gift cannot be earned; it's free.

You might illustrate this truth with your child's birthday. Most kids on their birthday receive one or more gifts. But as soon as they receive the gift, they don't go get their allowance so they can pay for it. You can't pay for a gift—it's free. All you have to do is receive it. Similarly, you can't buy the gift of salvation because God gives it to us. All we have to do is receive it. We receive this wonderful gift by placing our faith in Jesus. Placing faith in Jesus Christ is not complicated. It involves taking Christ at His word. Faith involves believing that Christ was who He said He was (God). It also involves believing that Christ can do what He claimed He could do— *He can forgive each one of us and come into our lives.*

5. *Allow your child to ask plenty of questions.* Children are naturally inquisitive. If you let them know they're allowed to ask questions about what you're saying, you can count on them to do so. Don't rush your discussion when sharing the gospel. Allow as much time as it requires.

6. *Lead your child in a simple prayer.* The prayer might go something like this:

Dear Jesus:

I want to have a relationship with you and get to know you.

I know I can't save myself because I know I'm a sinner.

Thank You for dying on the cross for me and taking the punishment for my sins.

I believe You died for me, and I accept Your free gift of salvation.

Thank You, Jesus.

Amen.

Ask your child if he (or she) really believes what he just said to God in prayer. If he does, he is now saved. He is a Christian. Tell him that the angels in heaven are cheering right now because he became a Christian (Luke 15:10).

One of the greatest blessings of salvation is that those who believe in Jesus are adopted into God's forever family (Romans 8:14,15). Close by emphasizing to your child how great it is to belong to *two* families—your family and God's forever family.

2

Teaching Your Children

"If you think education is expensive, try ignorance."

—*Anonymous*

A young boy once approached his father and asked, "Dad, why does the wind blow?"

The father responded, "I don't know, son."

"Dad, where do the clouds come from?"

"I'm not sure, son."

"Dad, what makes a rainbow?"

"No idea, son."

"Dad, do you mind me asking you all these questions?"

"Not at all, son. How else are you going to learn?"

Our children today need answers. And the most important answers we can provide are those that come from the pages of Scripture.

We noted at the beginning of chapter 1 that Timothy had been studying the Scriptures "from infancy" (2 Timothy 3:15). Timothy was not unique. Educating children in the ways of the Lord was a top priority in ancient Jewish culture. Among the Jews, the child was considered the most important person in the community. They believed that out of all the people on earth, the child was most dear to the heart of God. Understandably, then, educating children was considered a monumentally important task.

In fulfilling this task, the Jews didn't simply send their kids off to school and leave everything in the hands of teachers. Rather, the parents played the critical role. In fact, the Jews believed that the home was the absolute center of education for children. Certainly the Jews considered schools important, but schools cannot take the place of parents. As Jewish scholar Isidore Epstein observes, "In no other religion has the duty of the parents to instruct their children been more stressed than in Judaism."[1] This stress on educating children is not something the Jews just decided for themselves. Rather, as we will see in what follows, God Himself commanded parents to educate their children in the ways of the Lord.

All Jewish parents' desire for their children's education is encapsulated in Proverbs 1:8, which portrays a father speaking to his son: "Listen, my son, to your father's instruction and do not forsake your mother's teaching." By parental instruction, children were trained in the art of godly living. And then, as the children grew to adulthood, they would be prepared to train their children just as they had been trained. This is God's ideal.

A Mandate from God

In Deuteronomy 6:6-9, we read God's instructions regarding the spiritual education of children. In this passage, we see just how high a priority this education is with God:

> These commandments that I give you today are to be upon your hearts. Impress them on your children. Talk about them when you sit at home and when you walk along the road, when you lie down and when you get up. Tie them as symbols on your hands and bind them on your foreheads. Write them on the doorframes of your houses and on your gates.

The word "impress" in this passage literally means "to whet." We are to whet our children's appetites for the things of God. Our goal is to make the things of God palatable to our children so they will grow in their desire for them. The word "impress" is also a present-tense word. This means that the impressing is to be a continuous activity. It's not just a Sunday thing. It's a seven-day-a-week thing.

There is a secondary meaning of the word "impress": to sharpen. We are to sharpen our children's minds with God's laws so their thinking patterns will reflect His will. As we continue to impress the things of God upon our children's minds, they will increasingly build a Christian worldview— a grid through which they will see and interpret everything around them.

Every Christian child should learn how to interpret his culture "Christianly." Scripture is our lens through which we see all else. A clear-cut knowledge of God's Word will do more than anything else to form a Christian worldview in our children. A primary goal of teaching children is to expose them to the world, as revealed through the eyes of God, and to instill in them solid defenses against conformity to the fallen world of the secular community. Scripture instructs, "Do not conform any longer to the pattern of this world, but be transformed by the renewing of your mind" (Romans 12:2).

Christian educationalist Lawrence Richards warns us, "The child *will* build a worldview with the data he has . . . and if theological and moral content is not part of his data bank, his construct of reality will leave it out!"[2]

Loving God: Foundational to All Else

The context for the words about educating our children in Deuteronomy 6:6-9 is set in verse 5: "Love the LORD your God with all your heart and with all your soul and with all your strength." This is *the* foundational truth we must teach our kids as they grow up. Their supreme love—regardless of all the things that contend for their affections—must be for God alone.

Now, I want you to notice something here. The words in verse five are spoken directly to the parents. In other words, it's not just that we teach our kids to love God supremely. First and foremost, this verse is commanding *parents* to love God supremely. We cannot pass on to our children a love for God that we ourselves do not possess.

The late pastor Ray Stedman was right in emphasizing that "we can't expect our children to be changed unless something has changed us," and that "we can only communicate what we ourselves have discovered." He urged, "We must start with ourselves. And then we are responsible to pass on to our children what we have been taught and have learned and discovered in our own experience."[3]

The method we are to use in teaching our children is to relate what the Scriptures say to the context of *all of life*—when you sit down, when you walk around, when you lie down, and when you rise up. As you go about your day in the normal circumstances of life, teach your children about God and loving God.[4] God must be recognized everywhere in life.

The Christian home ought to be a place where God is present in our lives just as salt is present in the sea. It should be utterly natural and normal to talk about God—to relate to Him and to break into prayer at any moment.

The Teaching–Application Connection

Be a doer, not just a hearer.

The mere teaching of the Scriptures to our children is not enough. We must make sure they translate the teaching into application and transformation. This is the obvious instruction of Deuteronomy 31:12: "Assemble the people—men, women and children . . . so they can listen and learn to fear the LORD your God and *follow carefully all the words of this law*" (emphasis added).

Please notice that there are three reasons given for gathering the people (including children) together:

1) so they can listen to God's instructions

2) so they can learn to fear (or reverence) the Lord

3) so they can obey God's commandments.

Notice also that listening and learning are listed as separate items. Do you see significance in this? I do. A clear implication is that one can listen without learning. In other words, a person can hear God's instructions, but that doesn't necessarily mean he or she will follow those instructions and translate them into daily application.

As we teach our children, we must continually emphasize the difference between knowing something and applying it to our lives. It is not enough that our kids' heads get filled with Bible knowledge. The instructions from Scripture must be translated into daily life and applied (see Colossians 1:9,10).

Sharing Time: A Recipe for Action

Suppose I were wishing I had some delicious homemade chocolate-chip cookies. How can I make this wish come true? What must I do first?

First, I must get a chocolate-chip cookie recipe. Do I have cookies yet? No, not yet.

Next, I'll get my ingredients together—flour, sugar, butter, salt, soda, eggs, vanilla, and chocolate chips. Now do I have cookies? Not yet.

Next, I'll get out my big mixing bowl, my cookie sheets, my measuring cups, and my spoons. Do I have cookies yet? You're right—I don't.

Why not? I have everything I need for cookies—a recipe, ingredients, and dishes. What needs to happen next? I bet you know.

Of course—I have to *make* them! I have to *apply* the recipe. I have to *do* it!

It's not enough to have the directions and all the materials. If I want homemade cookies in my life, I must make them. We have to be "doers" of the recipe.

So it is with Scripture. We should be doers of what God asks, not just hearers!

3

Training Your Children

"The home is God's built-in training facility."[1]

—*Charles Swindoll*

Well-adjusted kids don't just happen. That's why God continually stresses in His Word the necessity of bringing our kids up and training them in the ways of the Lord. Only with consistent training will they become competent and healthy individuals grounded in God's principles.

Solomon, the wisest man who ever lived, gives us God's wisdom when he says, "Train a child in the way he should go, and when he is old he will not turn from it" (Proverbs 22:6). This verse is packed with applicational gems.

The word "train" comes from a word root that means "palate" or "roof of the mouth." The ancient Arabs used a form of this verb to denote the action of a midwife rubbing the palate of a newborn child with olive oil or crushed dates to give it a desire for food. The word connotes the idea of "creating a desire for" or "creating a taste for."[2] Proverbs 22:6 thus calls on Christian parents to develop in a child a personal desire for the things of God—a hunger for His Word and a desire for fellowship with His people.

If the child at a young age is given a desire for the Lord and His ways—if he "tastes" the reality of genuine godly experiences and the joy of following God's Word—he will not want to turn aside from his spiritual heritage when he reaches adulthood. It will stick with him for his entire life. We might paraphrase the verse this way: "Create a taste for the things of the Lord in your child, and even when he becomes mature he will not depart from his spiritual training."

Training: A Step Beyond Teaching

A thorough teacher goes a step beyond teaching to training. Training involves supervised "on the job" application of what has been taught. You and I, as parents, are called to be trainers, not just teachers. Kathi Hudson wrote a helpful book entitled *Raising Kids God's Way*. In it she recounts a story told by her father that perfectly illustrates the difference between teaching and training. Consider the words of this man:

> Since World War II, I've been a trained commercial pilot with an instrument rating. Because of my good training and extensive experience, I could sit a young, 21-year-old man in a classroom and teach him: FAA and Naval Regulations; navigation; aircraft ordinance; mechanical indoctrination, and radio procedures. He could pass all the examinations just fine. He would have had good, conscientious teaching.
>
> However, if I were to put him in a new jet fighter plane, pat him on the helmet, and say, "Have a nice flight, son," what would happen? It is likely he would crash and burn before he ever got off the runway. Why? He had good teaching but no training.
>
> Training always involves teaching, but teaching seldom includes training. Teaching with actual flight training would have saved the young pilot's life and the $15 million fighter plane. Training would insure him of a good future in flying. So it is with our children. They need for us to follow God's plan of training.
>
> To train this young man, I would take him on flights where I piloted, so I could model proper procedure. Then I would fly with him—giving him some independence but being there to offer advice and handle emergencies. Through this process, he would learn how to make important decisions, gain experience, and have complete control of his flight.

Only after a great deal of practice in the air would he be trained for a solo flight. Then, as situations arose he would automatically respond properly because of his extensive practical training. He'd be on human autopilot. He would automatically do the right thing, from good training.[3]

Developing Autopilot Responses

Training our children in the ways of the Lord helps them develop "autopilot" responses. As they encounter various circumstances (and temptations) in life, their childhood instruction in the ways of the Lord automatically kicks in and helps them make the right decisions.[4]

Now, here's something for you to think about. Whether you realize it or not, *you've been training your child from the moment he (or she) was born*.[5] Whether for good or for bad, you've been training your child by what you've modeled for him. He's an observer and an imitator. He puts into practice what he sees you do. He mimics your modus operandi in solving problems and handling life's challenges.[6]

Since this is the case, I'm sure you see the wisdom of taking a carefully planned approach to training your children. Just as a pilot instructor has a well-planned agenda in teaching his students, so we as parents need to have a well-planned agenda in training our kids in the ways of the Lord.[7] Our trainer manual is the Word of God. This book contains everything we need to know about God's will and a life of holiness. As 2 Timothy 3:16,17 puts it, "All Scripture is God-breathed and is useful for teaching, rebuking, correcting and training in righteousness, so that the man of God may be thoroughly equipped for every good work."

Training for Responsible Independence

As trainers, one of our goals is to increasingly enable our children to confront life's challenges with responsible independence. Children are only with us for a certain number of years, and after that they're on their own. When they leave the safe haven of home, they need to be ready to fly it alone.

You might look at it this way. When your child is helping you in the garden, you provide him with tools but you don't do all the digging for him, right? If we did all the digging for our child, he wouldn't learn anything about gardening. We model for our child how to use the tools, but we don't do the work for them.

In the same way, when training our children for life we give them tools for living, but we don't do all the digging for them. Otherwise they learn nothing. They need to increasingly become skilled in confronting life's challenges with responsible independence (but being carefully supervised by us the entire time).[8] This way, when it comes time for our child to leave home, making responsible, independent choices is not a new experience but is rather something our child already has a great deal of experience in. This way he doesn't crash land upon takeoff but rather soars with confidence into the wild blue yonder.

Modeling for Your Children

"Parents should first cultivate their souls
that in turn they may cultivate the souls
of their children."[1]

—*Billy Graham*

As young Johnny reached for the ringing phone one Saturday, his dad sighed through his teeth: "If it's the guy from the office, tell him I'm not home."

That evening the family went out for dinner. Before leaving the restaurant, Johnny's mother looked at the check and mentioned that the waitress had undercharged them.

"That's their tough luck," mumbled the father.

On the way home, they joked about the box that dad had bought for the dashboard of the car. He called it the "fuzz buster" and bragged that it had already paid for itself considering the speeding tickets he might otherwise have received.

Later that night, as Johnny finished his Sunday school lesson, he contemplated what a good Saturday it had been. How much better than last weekend when his father had grounded him for cheating on his arithmetic test.[2]

For Better or For Worse . . .

A contributor to *Reader's Digest* wrote about how he studied the Amish people in preparation for an article on them. In his observation at the schoolyard, he noted that the children never screamed or yelled. This amazed him.

The author spoke to the schoolmaster. He remarked how he had not once heard an Amish child yell, and asked why this was so. The schoolmaster replied, "Well, have you ever heard an Amish adult yell?"

Children are naturally great imitators. For better or for worse, they mimic adult behavior all the time. Jesus said "a student is not above his teacher, but everyone who is fully trained will be *like his teacher*" (Luke 6:40, emphasis added). As parents, you and I are our children's most important teachers. And whether we like it or not, they will become like their most important teachers—*us*!

I can think of many examples in Scripture in which a child mimicked the bad behavior of his parents:

- Isaac followed his father Abraham's negative example in deception (Genesis 12:12,13; 26:6-11).

- Jacob followed his father Isaac's negative example in unequal love for children (Genesis 25:27,28; 37:3,4).

- Ahaziah "did evil in the eyes of the LORD, because he walked in the ways of his father and mother" (1 Kings 22:52). His mother "encouraged him in doing wrong" (2 Chronicles 22:3).

- In Jeremiah 9:14 we read of those who "followed the Baals, as their fathers taught them."

By contrast, there are also many examples in Scripture of parents being good models for their children:

- "The LORD was with Jehoshaphat because in his early years he walked in the ways his father David had followed. He did not consult the Baals" (2 Chronicles 17:3).

- Uzziah "did what was right in the eyes of the LORD, just as his father Amaziah had done" (2 Chronicles 26:4).

- The apostle Paul said to young Timothy, "I have been reminded of your sincere faith, which first lived in your grandmother Lois and in your mother Eunice and, I am persuaded, now lives in you also" (2 Timothy 1:5).

Our children are watching what we do and how we act. Our behaviors are reflected in their behaviors. This means that we as parents need not only to quote Scripture, but also to live Scripture before our children. Revealed truth needs to be incarnated truth for it to make an impact on our children. Never forget that the way you live your life is the primary message your child receives.[3] Your convictions are caught more than taught.

Ingredients of a Good Model

As a parent, my goal is to be the best possible model for my children, David and Kylie. Ever since my seminary days, I've been convinced that the best summary of what makes a good model is that formulated by Christian education expert Lawrence Richards. Consider the following "ingredients" for a good model:

1. There needs to be frequent, long-term contact with the model(s).

2. There needs to be a warm, loving relationship with the model(s).

3. There needs to be exposure to the inner states [or feelings] of the model(s).

4. The model(s) need to be observed in a variety of life settings and situations.

5. The model(s) need to exhibit consistency and clarity in behaviors and values.

6. There should be a correspondence between the model's behavior and his expressed beliefs.

7. There should be an explanation in words of the model's lifestyle. That is, models need to *tell* as well as *show* the truths and principles that guide their actions.[4]

These seven points carry tremendous relevance for the relationship of parents to their children. I hope you make these points a part of your life fabric. No parent is 100-percent successful as a model, but I believe these seven points are the ideal to work toward.

We Should Model Our Failures, Too

As parents, all of us blow it from time to time in our attempt to be good models for our children. What do we do when we botch it royally? I believe we need to model the proper actions to take after we've messed up. Don't be timid about being open with your children when you blow it. Our children will learn from us even in our failures. They will discover how to handle their failures as they observe how we handle our failures.

Remember—as parents we are models not of perfection but of an ongoing process. In allowing our children to see our weaknesses, they will also be given the opportunity to see Jesus' strength working through our weaknesses (see John 15:5). As our children witness the transformation we are presently going through, it will help them see things in a proper light when they blow it.

Now that our foundation for teaching is finished, we will be focusing our attention on biblical principles you need to teach—and model for—your children.

Heaven Help the Home

1

Love and Time—Ties That Bind

"What we love to do we find time to do."[1]
—*John Spalding*

In 1991 Dr. Armand Nicholi, a respected professor at the Harvard Medical School and a staff physician at Massachusetts General Hospital, affirmed that "our family experience is the most significant experience of our lives. No human interaction has greater impact on our lives than our family experience."[2] Nicholi is right. And any book that sets out to address what children should know about God and the Bible must inevitably focus some heavy attention on the family.

In his presentation, Nicholi spoke of how the breakdown of the family in America contributes significantly to the major problems confronting our society. "Research data make unmistakably clear a strong relationship between broken families and the drug epidemic, the increase in out-of-wedlock pregnancies, the rise in violent crime, and the unprecedented epidemic of suicide among children and adolescents."[3] If we want to have healthy children, we must of necessity make the family unit a top priority.

Try as we may, though, our efforts at building a healthy family will be frustrated if we do not involve the Lord every step of the way. Scripture affirms, "Unless the LORD builds the house, its builders labor in vain" (Psalm 127:1). This means that our families, if they are to prosper and succeed in the way God intended, must be built upon the foundation of the Lord.

 We must follow God's formula and seek His involvement for family fulfillment.

The Gift of Love

As we look to the Scriptures for wisdom on the family, it quickly becomes apparent that the greatest gift we can give our children is the gift of love (Titus 2:4). Our children, at the core of their being, need to experience, see, and hear that they are unconditionally loved, accepted, and appreciated. Unconditional love—

> is loving a child no matter what. No matter what the child looks like. No matter what his assets, liabilities, and handicaps are. No matter what we expect him to be, and most difficult, no matter how he acts. This does not mean, of course, that we always like his behavior. Unconditional love means we love the child even when at times we may detest his behavior.[4]

There are so many ways we can show love to our children. In fact, to properly cover the subject would require book-length treatment. Here our goal is simply to highlight some of the more crucial components of loving children. Good books are available for those seeking a more detailed treatment.[5]

To begin, our children must be shown love and acceptance in both word *and* action. While it is absolutely necessary to say "I love you," there must also be physical expressions of that love in the form of affectionate touch. A hug, a kiss, a squeeze, and a hair-tousling are all little ways of expressing much love. It also says a lot to your children when you attend events that are important to them. Does your child participate in community soccer or baseball programs? If so, make every effort to attend most or all of those games. Do your children participate in gymnastics? Then by all means visit the gym and tell them how impressed you are. This tells them you love them.

Make it a point to know and stay up on your children's teachers, friends, current interests, fears, wishes, favorite foods, favorite colors, favorite books, favorite songs, and the like. Keeping up-to-date on this ever-changing list is another way of saying "I love you." It shows your children that you're interested in them.

I was reading a book entitled *How to Really Love Your Child* by Ross Campbell. He emphasized that a key means of expressing love to our children is *focused* attention.[6] Focused attention involves giving attention to our child in such a way that he feels important and unconditionally loved. It involves direct eye contact, undistracted time, and expressions of heartfelt interest in your child and his activities. Focused attention tells your child, "I like spending time with you." Campbell says we should seize the moment whenever the opportunity arises to give our child focused attention. This will make an impact on him or her that will stay with them for life.

Sometimes it may seem to parents that their attempts at focused attention are not yielding any positive results with their child. *But know that it is!* I read about a famous humanitarian whose diary spoke of a day he went fishing with his son. He lamented that the day was a total loss because his son seemed bored and preoccupied, saying very little. Years later, another historian compared this with an entry for that same day in the son's diary, which exclaimed what a perfect day it had been spending all that time alone with his father.[7]

The Myth of Quality Time

Journalist Russell Chandler reports, "Some statistics indicate that many teenagers spend an average of less than 30 minutes a week in a 'meaningful relationship' with their mothers and 15 minutes a week with their fathers."[8] Such statistics are appalling.

Don't think for a minute that kids don't notice it when you choose not to spend time with them. One study of 2,400 fifth graders indicated that the one thing they found most upsetting was that they didn't get to spend enough time with their parents.[9] "What really tears a kid up is not that you don't have more time, but *what* you choose to do when you do have time. Do you make the decision, 'I want to spend my time with you'?"[10]

One family counselor said, "Kids need intimate interaction with their parents. Ten minutes of superficial conversation around the dinner table won't do it."[11] Another counselor commented, "If our parents devoted the same amount of time to their children as they do some of their hobbies and shopping, today's kids would be transformed in a generation."[12]

Popular author Charles Swindoll once found himself with too many commitments in too few days. He got nervous and tense about it. "I was snapping at my wife and our children, choking down my food at mealtimes, and feeling irritated at those unexpected interruptions through the day. Before long, things around our home started reflecting the pattern of my hurry-up style. It was becoming unbearable.

"I distinctly remember after supper one evening, the words of our younger daughter, Colleen. She wanted to tell me something important that had happened to her at school that day. She began hurriedly, 'Daddy, I wanna tell you somethin' and I'll tell you really fast.'

"Suddenly realizing her frustration, I answered, 'Honey, you can tell me—and you don't have to tell me really fast. Say it slowly.'

"I'll never forget her answer: 'Then listen slowly.' "[13]

Parent-Parent Intimacy:
Your Child's Security Blanket

As we address the issue of love in the family unit, it is crucial that parents recognize how utterly important their own love for each other is to their children. Children derive immense benefit in seeing that mom and dad have a deep commitment and love for each other.

Dr. Howard Hendricks tells this story:

> I had a student come to me and say, "I have a problem. I love my wife too much."
>
> I blinked. "Run that by again. I hear it so seldom."
>
> I took him to the Ephesians passage: "Love your wife as Christ also loved the Church."
>
> "Do you love her that much?" I asked.
>
> "Oh, no, of course not!"
>
> I said, "Get with it!"[14]

The single most important relationship in any family is the marital relationship. It takes primacy over all other relationships—including the parent-child relationship. All of the above comments regarding expressions of love—the words, the affectionate touches, the interest in what's important to the other, the focused attention, the time spent together—all of these must first and foremost be directed to one's spouse!

You see, the parent-child bond is largely dependent on the quality of his parents' marital bond. A child's most basic security is in knowing his parents love each other. He is assured by this that he will never be abandoned and that he is a part of a strong, satisfying relationship. It is in such a family that parent-child intimacy is free to grow and flourish.

2

Making the Most of Family Devotions

"The family that *prays* together *stays* together."

—*Anonymous*

Charles Spurgeon, one of recent history's greatest preachers, said:

> I cannot tell you how much I owe to the custom on Sunday evenings while we were yet children for Mother to stay at home with us, and then we sat around the table and read verse after verse and she explained the Scriptures to us.... Then came our mother's prayer; and some of the words of our mother's prayer we shall never forget even when our hair is gray.[1]

Do family devotions really make a difference in the lives of our children? *Unequivocally yes!* Spurgeon is not unique. Countless people the world over have testified to the positive spiritual impact made during family time spent in Scripture. Many children have ended up in a life of ministry partially due to these special times in childhood.

Earlier in this book, we saw that learning about God and His ways should take place primarily in the home (Deuteronomy 6:6-9). And there's no time like a family devotional to come together and learn about God and His ways. I'm convinced, though, that the devil will do all he can to thwart your efforts. He hates family devotions. It goes against his purposes. He seems to pull out all the stops and drops everything in his arsenal on people to discourage family study. *Don't give him the victory.* Stand strong. God *will* bless your efforts!

Why Have a Family Devotional?

If you've never had a family devotional before, you might be more than a little hesitant, thinking that it is doomed to failure. You may be thinking, "It will be worse than a boring church service" or "What will I say?" or "What will we do?" Perhaps you think it won't be worth the effort to even try. But when you consider the purpose and benefits of family worship, I think you'll agree with me that it can only be good for your family.

One Christian child-education expert suggests that the purpose of family devotions includes the following:

- To promote family unity and love.

- To instruct the family in Christ's truth and to grow together in faith.

- To encourage communication within the family.

- To pray and rejoice together.

- To integrate biblical principles learned at church with school and home life; to enable us to live our faith in a practical manner.

- To develop a truly Christian spirit of love, yielding our individual rights as servants to one another.

- To fellowship together and have fun as a family.

- To instill in each member a desire to grow closer to the Lord.[2]

Sound good? I thought so. Perhaps the above list gives us a clue as to why the devil opposes family devotions so much. He stands against anything that can bring about so much good to so many people. Don't let him discourage you from making the effort!

Now, if you're married and your spouse is not a believer or is unwilling to participate, you may wonder if one parent alone can lead in family devotionals. *Absolutely!* Take the lead and have special spiritual times with your kids. These special get-togethers will pay rich dividends. But be sure not to let them become a point of contention in your marriage. Ask God for guidance in this area. Silently pray for your spouse's deliverance and understanding.

A Devotional Game Plan

Once you decide to have family devotionals, the next thing to do is to plan them.[3] Relax! The plan doesn't have to be complicated. Family devotions can be short and simple. In fact, it's best to keep them short and simple.

Here are some suggested components to a family devotional time:

1. Pick a designated time. Have each family member block that time open.

2. Have someone (a parent or older child at first) commit the time to God with an opening prayer.

3. Read some Scripture together. (The Gospels are a good place to start.)

4. Talk about what the verse or passage means and how it can apply to our lives.

5. Work on a memory verse together.

6. Read a page from a children's devotional. Look up and read related Bible verses.

7. Have a short time of worship. If someone in your family plays the piano or guitar, draft him or her for service. If there are no musicians in your family, don't let that stop

you. Singing without instruments can be great fun and very meaningful. Another idea is to sing along with worship tapes.

8. Have a time of prayer. Use the following acronym as a guide:

   A – Adoration (to God for who He is)

   C – Confession (of sin)

   T – Thanksgiving (for what God has done for you)

   S – Supplication (ask God for specific needs)

9. Close with a fun activity. Options include:

   • Play "What Bible character am I thinking of?" (Give clues.)

   • Play the Bible version of "Trivial Pursuit."

   • Do some Bible crossword puzzles (available from your Christian bookstore).

   • Tell some religious jokes. (My friend Bob Phillips has plenty of Christian humor books available.)

10. Optional: Be open to special projects that you can participate in as a family. For example:

    • You might occasionally have family members draw names out of a hat to do a secret nice deed that week for the family member they drew.[4]

    • You might decide as a family to support a missionary organization that feeds children. If you do this, you can put the picture of the child you're assigned on the refrigerator door and have regular prayer time for him or her during your devotionals.

    • Consider going to a Christian concert together. This can be a great time of bonding.

    • Go together to special programs offered at your church—or other churches in your area.

    • You might on occasion view a Christian video together. There are lots of good choices available for rent at your local Christian bookstore.

- Around Christmastime you might go shopping as a family for a bag of groceries and secretly put it on the doorstep of a needy family.

- You might participate as a family in helping an older couple paint their house or clean out their garage.

These are just a few of the special things you can do as a family to enhance your family sense of devotion to Christ.

Now, as you start having devotionals, keep in mind that it may take a few times to see what works best for your family. If your two-year-old toddles off down the hall or your ten-year-old refuses to sing, don't become discouraged or, worse, angry. Remember that there are spiritual forces at work here to thwart your enthusiasm. Adjust the "what" and the "how long" as needed until you find what works best for your family. Hang in there. God will bless your efforts and time spent gathered in His name!

Keep Prayer Journals

One last thing. I highly recommend that you give everyone in the family a little notebook for recording prayer requests. Put both an "Ask" column and an "Answer" column in each of them. This is a good way to keep track of God's answers to your prayers. There are two key benefits to this.

- First, it keeps your family prayers organized.

- Second, it helps kids see that God really does answer prayers. This is an important lesson that will stick with them throughout life. A record of answered prayers is a great faith-builder.

3

Boundaries of Love—Family Rules

"Let thy child's first lesson be obedience."[1]
—*Benjamin Franklin*

I read a story about a father named Jim who put his son Paulie to bed. After a few minutes Paulie called his father and asked for *another* drink of water.

Dad said, "No, go to sleep."

After several minutes, Paulie appealed again for a glass of water. Jim was more irritated this time. He spoke sharply and advised his son to forget it. But the boy would not be put off. He waited for a few minutes and then reopened the case.

Every time Paulie called his dad, Jim became more irritated. Finally, he said, "If you ask for water one more time I'm going to come in there and spank you!"

That quieted the boy for about five minutes, and then he said, "Daddy, when you come in here to spank me would you bring me a glass of water, please?" The kid got the water. He did not get the spanking.[2]

It is not surprising that when the Duke of Windsor was asked what impressed him most in America, he replied, "the way American parents obey their children."[3]

Rules and obedience. These are not words that most children like to talk about. But learning obedience is crucial for their well-being and happiness for the rest of their lives (not to mention the well-being and happiness of parents!).

God's Authority Structure

Foundationally, it is important for your child to understand that God is the one who set up authority structures among human beings. He set up the authority structure in the family.

> Everyone must submit himself to the governing authorities, for there is no authority except that which God has established. The authorities that exist have been established by God. Consequently, he who rebels against the authority is rebelling against what God has instituted, and those who do so will bring judgment on themselves (Romans 13:1,2).

The authority of parents, then, is not an authority of their own taking, but is one given them by God. Of course, it is the natural tendency for humans of all ages to balk at authority and rules. But, hopefully, as our children grow and mature, they will come to recognize that family rules are there for their protection and well-being.

Two Equal and Opposite Dangers

When it comes to setting family rules, parents must guard against two dangers. On one hand, we must guard against the danger of not setting any consistent rules at all. On the other hand, we must guard against the danger of an over-supply of petty regulations.[4] There is a balance that must be found and constantly checked. (This book will help you find that balance.)

Whenever possible—and according to the ages of your children—it is good to often remind them of the *reason* behind the rule. This doesn't mean you have to give an explanation for every instruction you give, but it is helpful to give the reasons behind the consistent family rules you've made.

Your children, over time and as they grow up, will begin to see the merit behind the rules and be able to apply them in other areas of life both inside the home and out.

 Honor your father and mother that it may go well with you.

Every parent must decide what rules are appropriate for their families. In our family, there are some things we absolutely insist on. Naturally we have rules involving safety issues. But among the rules most diligently taught, trained, and modeled are those having to do with parental honor and respect—which includes obedience, respectful speech, and basic politeness. For us to neglect this area of parental honor and respect would be a great detriment to both us and our children.

The apostle Paul in Colossians 3:20 instructs, "Children, obey your parents in everything, for this pleases the Lord." Remind your children that their obedience to you brings a smile to the face of God. It *pleases* Him.

In Ephesians 6:1, Paul says, "Children, obey your parents in the Lord, for this is right." The verse doesn't say, "Children, obey your parents if you *think* they're right." It says, "Obey your parents in the Lord *for this is right.*" The child is not responsible for weighing and evaluating his parents' decisions, and then obeying those which he deems right and rejecting those he does not agree with. The child's responsibility is simply to obey.

Notice also the little phrase "in the Lord." Children are to obey, not because this is what their parents want so much as because this is what the Lord Jesus wants. Obedience to parents is the child's responsibility to Christ.[5] And they are instructed to do this in a way that *brings honor* to their parents (see Ephesians 6:2). It is not to be a begrudging kind of obedience. It is to be an honoring kind of obedience.

We've all read about the little boy whose mother wanted him to sit down but he wouldn't do it. Finally she took hold of him and sat him down in the chair. He looked up at her with defiance in his eyes and said, "You may make me sit down outside, but I'm still standing up inside!"[6]

This is not an honoring kind of obedience. It is a begrudging kind of obedience. Teach children to see the difference. Only the honoring kind of obedience is acceptable to God. Honoring obedience comes as the child learns to obey out of a love of doing right and pleasing God. This incredible transition progressively emerges as you continue to remind your children of the reasons behind the rules you uphold and, of course, as they grow in their knowledge and love of the Lord. *This is a matter to be bathed in prayer.*

When You Can Say Yes, Say Yes

There are some things that we as parents can have a little liberty on. If an issue comes up that does not involve a moral or safety issue but is rather a desire based on personal taste, in our family we tend to go along with a lot of those little things (sometimes gritting our teeth). This is, loosely speaking, a matter of "picking your battles."

Professor Howard Hendricks tells a true story that profoundly illustrates the importance of picking your battles:

> Some parents will send a kid to hell for two inches of hair. Oooh, they make this a federal case! I knew of a Christian couple who chased a son out of their home and told him never to return until he went to a barber shop. He never returned. They're still looking for him—and wishing they had made a better decision. If you're going to take a stand, be sure you take a stand on the crucial issues! Oh, the agony of a father saying, "That's the worst decision I ever made in my life."[7]

Certainly there are some issues you must take a stand on, such as respect and honor for parents. But there are other issues that you can take liberty with. Hair length or hairstyle is a perfect example. In the scheme of things, these kinds of issues just aren't that important. Another example has to do with clothing. Ideally, we like our children to always dress nicely. But we don't have an ironclad rule that says, "You will always—without exception—wear precisely the clothes that mom and dad think are the best choice for that day."

Sometimes my 6-year-old daughter puts on clothes so "interestingly matched" that even our cats stare at her. But she feels very strongly about wearing those clothes that day. So, okay, we can grin and bear it. If she feels that strongly about it, she can wear those clothes. But we also try to provide some guidelines on how to choose clothes that *do* match. That way, as our daughter continues to grow older, she progressively learns how to make appropriate decisions regarding clothing.

Larry Christenson tells a true story that illustrates how children can sometimes gain great wisdom when parents bend a little and allow their kids to make foolish decisions on small issues:

> Some friends of ours have eight children, and they all love ice cream. On a hot summer day, one of the younger ones declared that she wished they could eat nothing but ice cream. The others chimed agreement, and to their surprise the father said, "All right. Tomorrow you can have all the ice cream you want—nothing but ice cream!" The children squealed with delight, and could scarcely contain themselves until the next day.
>
> They came trooping down to breakfast shouting their orders for chocolate, strawberry, or vanilla ice cream—soup bowls full! Mid-morning snack—ice cream again. Lunch—ice cream, this time slightly smaller portions. When they came in for mid-afternoon snack, their mother was just taking some fresh muffins out of the oven, and the aroma wafted through the whole house.
>
> "Oh goody!" said little Teddy. "Fresh muffins—my favorite!" He made a move for the jam cupboard, but his mother stopped him.

"Don't you remember? It's ice cream day—nothing but ice cream."

"Oh, yeah . . ."

"Want to sit up for a bowl?"

"No thanks. Just give me a one-dip cone."

By supper time the enthusiasm for an all-ice-cream diet had waned considerably. As they sat staring at fresh bowls of ice cream, Mary—whose suggestion had started this whole adventure—looked up at her daddy and said, "Jeepers, couldn't we just trade in this ice cream for a crust of bread?"[8]

A valuable lesson learned! Remember—children tend to make judgments from an extremely small base of knowledge and experience. As they grow up, you can help them expand that base of knowledge and experience by allowing them to make a few (secretly supervised) foolish decisions.

A Prerequisite to Rule-Setting

A prerequisite to setting family rules is that your relationship with your children be one that is characterized by love and respect. Parents sometimes forget that relationships precede rules. The experts have long told us that a child tends to accept your ideas and philosophy because he accepts you. Conversely, he tends to reject your ideas and philosophy when he rejects you.[9]

Without a display of love on your part, your child will *react* to your rules rather than *act* upon them. If you want your children to take your rules seriously, then you need to take seriously their need to be loved. That's the way it works.

4

Teaching Responsibility

One of my little nephews (five years old) was given the responsibility of being the ring bearer at a friend's wedding. He took this responsibility very seriously. No doubt about it. When it came time for the rehearsal, his big moment arrived. He had to walk the aisle with the ring. At that moment, he raised his hands high in a claw-like stance, began growling ferociously, and started to make his way to the front. No one knew what to make of the spectacle until someone in the crowd realized he was acting like a bear. My nephew thought he was the "ring bear." He thought he was being responsible. You have to give him an "A" for effort.

Learning how to be responsible is a key lesson all our children must learn. But this is not a lesson that is taught all at once. It is taught progressively, over many years, with increased responsibility given as each year passes.

Learning to Count the Cost

Scripture says there are *always* consequences—good or bad—to our choices and actions.

> *"The righteousness of the blameless makes a straight*
> *way for them, but the wicked are brought down by*
> *their own wickedness"* (Proverbs 11:5).

Our kids must learn that there are always consequences to their choices and actions. If we constantly shield our kids from the consequences of their wrong choices, they will never learn not to do wrong. For this reason, it is important that our kids be allowed to suffer some of the consequences of their foolish actions (assuming the consequences don't involve physical harm). This is one of the ways they learn responsibility.

Sharing Time: The Wake-Up Call

One school-day morning, 10-year-old Johnny was hanging out in his bed. His mother had told him twice already to get up and get dressed for school, but he chose to stay in bed just a little longer. He knew his mom wouldn't let him be late for school. It was a scenario they'd played out umpteen times. . . .

Johnny would sleep late. Mom would beg, wheedle, cajole, and finally yell for Johnny to get up and get ready. She would get his clothes out of the dresser and bring them to him. She would pack his backpack for him. They'd both skip breakfast. Mom would put the pedal to the metal and weave in and out of traffic. They'd screech into school just in the nick of time.

Not today! Mom had wised up. She'd decided to put the responsibility back where it belonged—on Johnny. And she'd told him the night before that in the morning she would give him two (being generous) wake-up calls, and that the rest was his responsibility. He would get his own clothes, pack his own backpack, and mom would no longer be skipping breakfast or speeding to school.

Well, when Johnny finally got to school, he had to go to the principal's office to get a tardy slip. And when he arrived in his classroom, he found out he had already missed part of a lesson. He was embarrassed, and he was behind.

Did Johnny learn a good lesson? Yes, he did. He learned that there are consequences when you make bad decisions. From then on, Johnny decided he would be responsible and get up the first time he was told.

Sharing Time: Learning the Hard Way

Mommy told Sarah to be sure to put the lid on her Play-Doh when she finished playing with it because, if she didn't, the Play-Doh would dry up and become hard as a rock.

After playing with the Play-Doh for a while, Sarah decided she wanted to play with something else. So she left without putting the lid back on her Play-Doh. And just like her mommy said, the Play-Doh dried up and became hard as a rock.

When Sarah wanted to play with her Play-Doh the next day, was she sad? Yes, she was. She wished she had done what her mom said.

From then on, Sarah decided she would be responsible and take care of her Play-Doh.

Taking the Long Look

 Try to take "the long look" when making major decisions. Consider the long-term consequences of your actions.

"A prudent man gives thought to his steps" (Proverbs 14:15).

It is critically important that our kids learn to take the long look when it comes to their choices and actions. By learning to consider possible consequences, their decisions become increasingly responsible and wise. Kids can be taught that when they're contemplating an action they can first consider, "What might happen next if I do this?" The more this mindset is instilled in them, the more responsible they will become.

Sharing Time: Thinking Ahead

A little boy named Paul was riding his bike one day. As he was riding, his tire hit a stone. When that happened, he lost control of his bike, and he crashed on the side of the road.

Fortunately, Paul had a helmet on. Without that helmet, he would probably have seriously hurt his head and would have had to go to the hospital.

It turns out that Paul had put on his helmet without having to be told by his mom. Responsibility is doing what you should without being told. So Paul was being responsible.

Paul had taken the "long look." He knew that if he crashed without a helmet on, he might hurt his head. So he decided to wear a helmet.

Like Paul, we need to take the long look before making decisions. For example:

- If you throw a rock when you're around other people, what bad thing might happen next?

- If you're running around by the side of a swimming pool where it's wet and very slippery, what bad thing might happen next?

Before deciding to do things, we should consider, "What might happen next if I do this?"

Building a Virtuous Heart

1

Walking in Humility

"Humility is the exhibition of the spirit of Jesus Christ and is the touchstone of saintliness." [1]

—*Oswald Chambers*

Corrie ten Boom was once asked if it was difficult for her to remain humble. She replied quite simply:

> When Jesus rode into Jerusalem on Palm Sunday on the back of a donkey, and everyone was waving palm branches and throwing garments on the road, and singing praises, do you think that for one moment it ever entered the head of that donkey that any of that was for him?

Her point was, "If I can be the donkey on which Jesus Christ rides in His glory, I give him all the praise and all the honor."[2] What a beautiful picture of humility!

The Scriptures tell us that those who want to please God must walk in humility. In today's culture, which constantly promotes the look-out-for-number-one philosophy, it is crucial that our children learn the virtue of humility.

Honoring Someone Else

 Don't seek your own honor, but rather look for ways to honor others and be glad in their success.

"Honor one another above yourselves. . . . Rejoice with those who rejoice" (Romans 12:10,15).

God wants us to walk humbly and look for ways to honor others. He wants us to rejoice with others as they rejoice.

Sharing Time: Samuel's Trophy

Kyle had been playing on soccer and baseball teams for five years. Between these sports and school activities he had won 10 trophies. One day his younger friend and neighbor, Samuel, came up to him and said, "Kyle, guess what? I won a trophy! It's the first one I ever got in my whole life." He was very excited.

How would Samuel have felt if Kyle had said, "That's good, but I've got 10 trophies. What do you think of that?!" Would Kyle have been looking for a way to honor others or would he have been seeking honor for himself?

Thankfully Kyle didn't say that. Instead, he said, "Samuel, that's fantastic! I am so happy for you. Let me shake your hand!" That made Samuel feel great! Kyle had seen a wonderful opportunity to honor someone else and to be glad in his success.

Later, when Samuel found out how many trophies Kyle had, Samuel said, "Wow, Kyle, that's incredible! I'm happy for you too!"

God doesn't want us to seek our own honor.
He wants us to seek the honor of others.

God Exalts the Humble

God exalts those who are humble, but He humbles those who seek to exalt themselves.

"The LORD tears down the proud man's house" (Proverbs 15:25).

"He has brought down rulers from their thrones but has lifted up the humble" (Luke 1:52).

"Humble yourselves before the Lord, and he will lift you up" (James 4:10).

All through the Bible we see God exalting the humble and humbling those who exalt themselves.

- David humbled himself and God exalted him greatly by making him a king (2 Samuel 7:18-21).

- The apostle Paul humbled himself and God exalted him greatly, using him mightily to spread the gospel (1 Timothy 1:15,16; see also 1 Corinthians 15:9 and Ephesians 3:8).

- Uzziah, by contrast, became prideful and was unfaithful to the Lord, and this led to his downfall. God afflicted him with leprosy (2 Chronicles 26:16-18).

Sharing Time: An Angel's Pride

Once, a long time ago, God created the angels. One of them was very strong and very beautiful. He was called the "shining one." He was stronger and more beautiful than any of the other angels.

This angel became so impressed with his own greatness that he stopped giving worship and glory to God, His creator. He became so puffed up with his own magnificence that he demanded glory and worship for himself. He decided he was better than God, and wanted to take God's place.

God immediately judged this angel and cast him out of heaven. This is an example of how pride can lead to a downfall.

The Wardrobe of God's Children

Open your Bible and read to your child from 1 Peter 5:5: "Clothe yourselves with humility toward one another, because, 'God opposes the proud but gives grace to the humble.'" God wants us to "wear" humility. He wants our appearance to others to show humility, not pride. When other people see us, they should see us as a reflection of Jesus, who was humble and meek (Matthew 11:29).

2

A Willingness to Learn

"If you think you know it all, you haven't been listening."[1]

—*Anonymous*

Thomas D. Bailey, state superintendent of Florida schools, tells the story of two second-graders who were standing in the school playground during recess when a jet flew over.

"Look at that," said one lad, "it's a BX50."

"No, a BX51," said the other. "You can tell by its wing sweep."

"You're right," the first youngster conceded. "It's not going more than 760 miles per hour either, because it didn't break the sound barrier."

On this point they both agreed.

"It's amazing the pressure that develops on those planes when they go into a dive," the second boy said. "Almost 1,200 pounds per square inch."

At this point the bell called the children back to the classroom. The first boy turned to the second. "There's the bell," he sighed. "Let's go back in and finish stringing those beads."[2]

Today's kids are smart in a lot of things—and that's good. But they've still got a lot to learn, especially when it comes to living God's way. The problem, though, is that many children seem to have a built-in resistance to being taught anything. How often we parents hear, "I know, I know, you don't have to tell me," coming out of our kids' mouths! For this reason, the virtue of being teachable is among the most important traits we can hope to impart to them at an early age.

A Wise and Discerning Heart

Solomon was the wisest man who ever lived. But he wasn't born that way. Rather, recognizing his deficiency, he asked God to give him wisdom (read 1 Kings 3:2-15). And God granted his request. God told him:

> Since you have asked for this and not for long life or wealth for yourself, nor have asked for the death of your enemies but for discernment in administering justice, I will do what you have asked. I will give you a wise and discerning heart, so that there will never have been anyone like you, nor will there ever be (1 Kings 3:11,12).

Solomon was a teachable *person* even though He was the son of a king. He knew he didn't have the kind of wisdom he needed, so he asked God for it. And God made him incredibly wise. None of us, including our children, will ever become as wise as Solomon. But we need to teach our kids the scriptural truth that a key to growing wise and smart is to have a teachable attitude.

Those who are willing to listen and learn are those who will grow wise and succeed in life.

"He who listens to a life-giving rebuke will be at home among the wise. He who ignores discipline despises himself, but whoever heeds correction gains understanding" (Proverbs 15:31,32).

Scripture indicates that two foundational characteristics of the wise person are that *he listens* and *he is teachable*. The fool, in contrast, refuses to listen or learn and, accordingly, suffers many consequences.

Do you remember reading about Apollos in Scripture? Apollos was a man who knew a lot about God. But he needed to know more. When he met Priscilla and Aquila, a godly wife and husband, he went to their home and listened to them as they explained the things of God to him more fully. *Apollos was teachable.* His pride was not offended when they told him he needed to know more. Rather, he joyfully took the opportunity to learn more and gain more wisdom (Acts 18:24-28). We need to teach our children to be the same way.

There is a modern proverb that says, "We have two ears and one mouth; therefore, we should listen twice as much as we speak."[3] Our children need to understand the importance of being good listeners and being teachable.

Sharing Time: What About the Instructions?

Little Fred was so excited because his mom took him shopping, and he had bought a model of a jet. The model came in many pieces that would have to be glued together in the right way to make the jet.

When Fred got home he immediately dumped all the pieces of his model jet out of the box and started gluing them together. His dad said, "Whoa, slow down buddy! Let's look at these easy instructions on the box first to make sure you're doing it right."

But Fred said, "I know how to do it, Dad. I don't need the instructions."

Dad said, "I think we'd better look at the instructions so we do it right."

Fred said, "I don't want to. I already know how to do it."

Can you guess what happened? Fred ended up gluing wrong pieces together, and the glue dried. *The model was wrecked.*

Fred wasn't teachable, was he? If he had been, today he would have a great model jet. But because he wouldn't listen, his jet got ruined.

We need to always be teachable.

3

An Honest Heart

> "A commentary of the times is that the word *honesty* is now preceded by *old-fashioned*."[1]
>
> —*Larry Wolters*

A farmer's crop of melons was disappearing fast from his field. Thieves were continually stealing the melons under the cover of night's darkness. The farmer finally became desperate and, in an attempt to save his crop from the vandals (which he suspected were kids), he decided to put up a sign. The sign had a skull and crossbones on it, and it read: "One of these melons is poisoned." Only the farmer knew that it wasn't true.

Sure enough, for two nights not a single melon was missing. But after the third night, the farmer noticed that his sign had been altered. Someone had scratched out the word "one" and replaced it with another word so that the sign now read: "Two of these melons are poisoned."

Attempting to save his whole crop through a small deception, he lost it all. (Since he didn't know if the second melon had *really* been poisoned—and since he couldn't possibly know which one of the melons may have been poisoned—he had to destroy the whole crop.) This perfectly illustrates Sir Walter Scott's observation: "Oh, what a tangled web we weave, When first we practice to deceive!"[2]

Truth or Consequences

 God always wants us to tell the truth and not be deceptive in any way.

"A truthful witness gives honest testimony, but a false witness tells lies" (Proverbs 12:17).

"There are six things the LORD hates, seven that are detestable to him: haughty eyes, a lying tongue, hands that shed innocent blood, a heart that devises wicked schemes, feet that are quick to rush into evil, a false witness who pours out lies and a man who stirs up dissension among brothers" (Proverbs 6:16-19).

There is a great story in Scripture that illustrates the importance of honesty. Zacchaeus, a tax collector, was very wealthy. According to Roman law, tax collectors had to collect a certain amount of money from each person and give it to the Roman government. Often, though, they would charge a little extra and put that extra money into their own pockets.

Zacchaeus became a follower of Christ. And, in showing his sincerity, he said to Jesus, "Look, Lord! Here and now I give half of my possessions to the poor, and if I have cheated anybody out of anything, I will pay back four times the amount" (Luke 19:8). In becoming a Christian, Zacchaeus learned the importance of honesty!

It's good to learn honesty as an adult—but it's much better to learn it as a child.

Sharing Time: Chocolate Cake and Stale Cookies

When Kerri was in second grade, she was a member of the Campfire Girls organization, in a group called the Bluebirds. Her Bluebird troop was having a meeting one evening to celebrate the birthday of one of the girls.

The girls were chatting, and the conversation moved to the subject of allergies. Many of the girls were naming particular things to which they were allergic. Kerri, not wanting to be the only one without allergies and wanting to fit in, announced that she was allergic to chocolate. (This was a total lie!)

That statement caught the ear of the troop leader mother in the next room, who was slicing (you guessed it) chocolate birthday cake. This was actually Kerri's favorite. Kerri—to cover her lie—had to make do with a few stale sugar cookies while the other girls enjoyed delicious chocolate cake.

Kerri learned a painful lesson that day. She learned the importance of being honest.

4

A Kind Heart

"Can you ever remember a time when
you regretted having said a kind word?"[1]
—*Anonymous*

Some years back, my family was out for an evening stroll around the block. My wife was pushing my then-infant daughter in the stroller and my three-year-old son, David, was toddling along with us.

In the preceding days, David and I had had several discussions prompted by his questions on the dangers of cigarette smoking. The topic was fresh on his mind.

As we rounded the corner, we came upon one of our neighbor acquaintances out on her front porch. She was smoking a cigarette. Before we could even wave hello, David gasped, pointed at her cigarette, and said, "You're gonna die!" She was speechless; we were mortified. Fumbling for words, I called out a weak "sorry" and mumbled something about "those three-year-olds," while my wife nudged David down the sidewalk posthaste.

On the way home, David and I had a heart-to-heart talk about kindness. A big part of the discussion was on the Golden Rule.

The Golden Rule

Always treat others in the way you would have them treat you.

"Do to others as you would have them do to you" (Luke 6:31).

Today's predominant philosophy is, "Do unto others before they do unto you." Contrary to this, we must teach our children the philosophy of Jesus found in Luke 6:31.

Sharing Time: A Good Rule to Remember

Emily Hunter, in her excellent book *A Child's First Steps to Virtues*, illustrates the Golden Rule this way:

> It was Jeff's first day at a new school. When he arrived home, his mother asked, "How was school?"
>
> "It was *awful!*" Jeff replied. "No one talked to me, no one ate lunch with me, no one played with me!"
>
> "Don't feel bad," his mother said, "you'll soon make new friends." Her words came true. In time Jeff made many new friends.
>
> One day another new boy arrived at school. His name was Steve. Jeff could see Steve felt lonely. Jeff remembered how he felt on his first day at the new school. He also remembered a Bible truth his dad had taught him—the "Golden Rule."
>
> "In any situation," his dad had said, "ask yourself this question: 'How would I want others to treat *me?*' Whatever your answer, son, that's how you should treat *others!*"
>
> Jeff remembered exactly how he had wanted others to treat him on his first day at the new school. He had wanted his new classmates to be friendly. Jeff decided, "I will be friendly to Steve." So he ate lunch with him, played ball with him, and waved a friendly goodbye to him when school was over.
>
> When Steve arrived home, his mother said, "How do you like your new school, Steve?"

"It was *great!*" he replied happily. "But at first I felt terribly lonely. Then a boy named Jeff made friends with me. *He seemed to know exactly how I was feeling!* It sure made a difference!"

That evening Jeff confided in his dad, "I'm glad you taught me the Golden Rule. I needed to remember that rule today."

Jeff's dad looked pleased. "It's a good rule to remember *every* day, son!"

Jeff nodded. He knew his dad was right![2]

The Good Samaritan

 When you see someone who needs help, you should try to be a Good Samaritan and help them.

A story in the Bible that you can use to show the importance of compassion and kindness is Jesus' parable of the Good Samaritan. Read Luke 10:30-37 to your child:

> Jesus said: "A man was going down from Jerusalem to Jericho, when he fell into the hands of robbers. They stripped him of his clothes, beat him and went away, leaving him half dead. A priest happened to be going down the same road, and when he saw the man, he passed by on the other side. So too, a Levite, when he came to the place and saw him, passed by on the other side. But a Samaritan, as he traveled, came where the man was; and when he saw him, he took pity on him. He went to him and bandaged his wounds, pouring on oil and wine. Then he put the man on his own donkey, took him to an inn and took care of him. The next day he took out two silver coins and gave them to the innkeeper. 'Look after him,' he said, 'and when I return, I will reimburse you for any extra expense you may have.'
>
> "Which of these three do you think was a neighbor to the man who fell into the hands of robbers?"
>
> The expert in the law replied, "The one who had mercy on him."
>
> Jesus told him, "Go and do likewise" (Luke 10:30-37).

Sharing Time: Helping Someone in Need

There was a new boy in school named Tom whose family had just moved to town from another state. It was hard for Tom starting out in a new school where he knew no one. But to make matters worse, he had a broken leg. There he was, dragging himself around on crutches trying to find his way in a strange building and carrying his books at the same time.

One day, between classes when there were hundreds of students in the hallway, Tom dropped all his books. He thought to himself, *Oh, no! How am I going to pick all these books up while I'm on crutches?*

Just then, a boy named Jim decided to stop and help Tom. He picked all the books up very quickly so no one stepped on them, and then he carried the books to Tom's next class for him.

Jim was being a Good Samaritan that day! He had seen an obvious opportunity to help someone in need and he took it. *We should be Good Samaritans too!*

5

A Generous Heart

"Giving is the thermometer of love." [1]
—*Anonymous*

I read a story about a chaplain who had set out to raise a million dollars for missions. Toward reaching this goal he encountered many disappointments. He often became discouraged. One day, while going through his mail, he came across a letter from a little boy. When he opened it, out fell a battered nickel. The letter, in a boyish scrawl and liberally punctuated with blots, said:

> Dear Chaplain:
> I'm sure you're going to get a million dollars for missions. And I'm going to help you get it too. So here's a nickel toward it. It's all I've got right now, but if you need any more, you just call on me.

This became the chaplain's most effective story in his money-raising campaign. Through it, he was eventually able to reach his goal. A boy's generous nickel, multiplied, became a million dollars. [2]

God Wants Us to Be Generous

God wants us to be generous toward others, just as He is generous toward us.

"Good will come to him who is generous and lends freely" (Psalm 112:5).

75

Charles Swindoll once said that "we are never more like God than when we give."[3] I think he is right. God displayed incredible generosity in sending His Son to save us. He shows His generosity every day as He showers His grace and mercy upon us. And as we show generosity to others, we reflect God in a tiny way.

Sharing Time: A Bag Full of Candy

Begin by reading Luke 12:16-21 to your child. Then say:

Steven went to the birthday party of a friend one Saturday morning. While at the party, they had a game to see who could break open the piñata with a stick while blindfolded. When it came time for Steven's turn, he managed to hit the piñata very hard. When it broke open, lots of candy fell out. Everyone dove for the candy with their bags. Steven ripped off his blindfold and managed to stuff lots of candy into his bag.

Wow, this will last me a long, long time! Steven thought to himself.

The next day he took his bag to Sunday school to brag and show all the other kids at church how much candy he had for himself. When it came time for the Sunday-school lesson, the teacher talked about the parable of the rich man who stored lots of grain and goods for himself without sharing with others. The rich man selfishly thought to himself, "This will last me a long, long time."

After hearing the lesson, Steven decided he didn't want to be like that rich man. Instead, he wanted to share what was his with others. So, after asking his teacher if it was okay, he opened his bag and gave everyone in his class some candy.

Steven was being generous!

A Little Boy's Generosity

There's a story in the New Testament where we witness a mighty miracle that occurred as a result of a little boy's generosity. It is found in John 6:1-14. Read this passage aloud to your child, and then read the following poem by Emily Hunter which summarizes the passage:

> "Little boy, little boy!
> I hesitate to ask it . . .
> Little boy, could you share
> Whatever's in your basket?"
>
> "Take it, sir! Take it, sir!
> It's just a tiny lunch.
> With all the many people here,
> It isn't very much."
>
> "There're only five small barley loaves
> And these two little fish.
> My mother fixed them just for me,
> But take them if you wish!"
>
> And as the little boy looked on,
> His eyes popped out of his head!
> For everyone had fish to eat
> And everyone had bread!
>
> For when the Savior took his lunch,
> And asked a blessing on it,
> Each time a piece was broken off,
> A new one grew upon it!
>
> Yes, everyone had lots to eat.
> Each person ate his fill.
> And when they all could eat no more,
> There were twelve baskets still![4]

We will likely not witness this kind of miracle when we're generous. But it always brings a smile to God when He sees His children displaying a giving attitude.

Help your child think through different ways he or she can be generous. For example:

- We can be generous with our toys when our friends come over.

- We can be generous with our time if we see a friend who is lonely.

- We can be generous with our help when we see mom or dad cleaning up the house.

- We can be generous at the playground by giving others a turn on the swing set.

6

Good Work Habits

"The Bible doesn't promise loaves to the loafer." [1]

—*Anonymous*

A virtue that is critical to each child's future success in life is having good work habits. If he or she learns this virtue early, it will stick with him or her throughout life and pay rich dividends.

 God rewards hard work.

"Each will be rewarded according to his own labor" (1 Corinthians 3:8).

"Whatever you do, work at it with all your heart, as working for the Lord, not for men" (Colossians 3:23).

God says that whatever kind of work we are involved in, we should do it with all our heart. He rewards hard work!

Sharing Time: The Little Red Hen

A great way to illustrate the importance of learning work is to use the classic story of the little red hen:

Once upon a time there was a little red hen, a fox, a dog,

and a pig. They decided they'd like to have some nice home-made bread.

The little red hen said, "First we must grow some wheat. Who will help me plant this wheat?"

"Not I," said the dog.

"Not I," said the fox.

"Not I," said the pig.

So the little red hen said, "Then I'll do it myself." And she did.

When it came time to harvest the wheat the little red hen asked, "Who will help me harvest this wheat?"

"Not I," said the dog.

"Not I," said the fox.

"Not I," said the pig.

So the little red hen said, "Then I'll do it myself. " And she did.

Then the little red hen said, "Who will help me pound this wheat into flour?"

"Not I," said the dog.

"Not I," said the fox.

"Not I," said the pig.

So the little red hen said, "Then I'll do it myself." And she did.

Then the little red hen said, "Who will help me bake this bread?"

"Not I," said the dog.

"Not I," said the fox.

"Not I," said the pig.

So the little red hen said, "Then I'll do it myself." And she did.

The smell of the homemade bread baking wafted outside to the attention of the dog, the fox, and the pig.

Then the little red hen said, "Who will help me eat this bread?"

The dog, the fox, and the pig came running.

"I will," said the dog.

"I will," said the fox.

"I will," said the pig.

"Oh no you won't," the little red hen said. "I asked you to help me plant the wheat. I had to do it myself.

"I asked you to help me harvest the wheat. I had to do it myself.

"I asked you to help me pound the wheat into flower. I had to do it myself.

"I asked you to help me bake this bread. I had to do it myself.

"Now it is time to eat this bread, and I'm going to eat it myself."

The fox, the dog, and the pig didn't want to work. And because they didn't do any work, they were sorry later. They didn't get any bread. There are rewards for hard work—and the little red hen got her reward.

God wants us to learn how to work. Then we won't have to be sad later like the dog, the fox, and the pig.

God's Appointment of Work

"Go to the ant, you sluggard; consider its ways and be wise! It has no commander, no overseer or ruler, yet it stores its provisions in summer and gathers its food at harvest" (Proverbs 6:6-8).

The ant makes a great teaching illustration for children. If you come across some busy ants in the lawn, seize the moment and illustrate the importance of work by watching the ants with your child (taking precautions not to get stung).

If you're lucky, you'll see some ants carrying objects that are bigger than they are. They are hard workers. God tells us to look at how hard the ants work and learn a lesson from them. Just as they work hard, God wants us to work hard. Here are some interesting facts from Scripture about work:

- God appointed man to work right after He created man (Genesis 2:15).

- It is by working that we obtain our daily provisions of food and support ourselves (2 Thessalonians 3:10).

- God desires that we find satisfaction in our work (Ecclesiastes 5:18-20).

- An important part of learning good work habits is being self-dependent—taking the initiative to do a good job by yourself (see 1 Thessalonians 4:11,12).

- God is our example in work. God worked for six days in creating the universe and then rested on the seventh day (Genesis 2:2,3).

- Jesus worked hard as a carpenter, a trade He learned from His father Joseph (Mark 6:3).

- The apostle Paul worked hard as a tentmaker. He spent a lot of his time in ministry, but he supported himself financially by making tents (Acts 18:3).

Teaching Your Child to Work

Below are five important factors to keep in mind when teaching your children to work.[2]

1. *Give your children hands-on instruction.* Don't assume your children know how to do the tasks you assign them. If you assign your child to clean out the garage, for example, go to the garage and demonstrate how to do it. Show them where the bikes go. Show them how to hang the tools. Show them how to sweep. Remember—kids learn by imitation.

2. *As much as possible, try to include in your children's work assignments a certain level of fun.* For example, when cleaning out the garage, let them bring a cassette player so they can listen to their favorite tapes as they work.

3. *Give them plenty of encouragement.* Compliment them when they've done a good job. Show appreciation. Try to make it a

positive experience and give them a sense of accomplishment. Remind them that they are contributing to the running of the household when they work. They'll remember this sense of fulfillment the next time they're assigned a task.

4. *When you assign your children a task, have a standard of excellence which requires them to do a good job.* They need to learn this standard of excellence in the home. This will be crucial to their success throughout their time in school as well as in their future careers. They may complain on occasion about this standard, but it will be well worth the effort.

5. *Start your child working at a young age.* Work should not take the place of fun and games. Allow plenty of time for fun, but also require some work assignments that are appropriate for their age. They can learn to tidy up their rooms, pick up their toys, put dirty clothes in a basket, dry the dishes, cut out coupons (with safety scissors), and other tasks such as these.

Quest for Success

1

Success God's Way

"Successful people are those who apply
God's remedy for failure." [1]

— *Erwin Lutzer*

A successful man was asked the secret of his accomplishments in the business world. He replied, "Good judgment."

"Where did you learn good judgment?" he was asked.

"From experience."

"And from where did you gain your experience?"

"From poor judgment." [2]

It is true that good judgment has a great deal to do with success in life. It is also true that one gains good judgment and wisdom from *the Scriptures*. That's one of the main points of this book.

The world offers numerous definitions of what it means to be successful. Some people say it involves the attainment of wealth, status, and power. Some measure it in terms of intellect. Some measure it in terms of physical appearance. Some measure it in terms of fame. Some measure it by the size of one's house. Scripture has an entirely different perspective. The Scriptures consistently tell us that God prospers those *who obey Him*. And prosper doesn't necessarily mean material wealth. Prosper can simply mean success in whatever endeavor you are engaged in.

In her helpful book *Raising Kids God's Way*, Kathi Hudson offers this definition of success: "Success is living in such a way that you are using what God has given you—your intellect, abilities, and energy—to reach the purpose that He intends for your life."[3] We should encourage our children to excel in the areas in which God has given them skills and abilities. We should not try to mold them into some preconceived image we have of what they should be.

Success in God's Eyes

 God wants you to be successful in life, to achieve the purpose for which you were created.

> *"Blessed is the man who does not walk in the counsel of the wicked or stand in the way of sinners or sit in the seat of mockers. But his delight is in the law of the LORD, and on his law he meditates day and night. He is like a tree planted by streams of water, which yields its fruit in season and whose leaf does not wither. Whatever he does prospers"* (Psalm 1:1-3).

Success in God's eyes is not at all similar to the version of success offered by the world. Our children must learn the difference between the two. Help them understand how to succeed according to God's standards, not according to the standards of the world.

Sharing Time: RoboMan

Professor Gizmo was a toy inventor who worked for the PlayCo Toy Company. He had just been assigned a new project by his boss.

"Professor," said the boss, "we need you to invent a new robot. We want this robot to do five things: 1) roll forward,

2) roll backward, 3) roll sideways, 4) say, "I'm RoboMan," and 5) flash colored lights on his chest. Do you think you can make a robot do these five things?"

The professor nodded. "I can make the robot you need, boss. I'll get right to work."

Professor Gizmo got busy and worked and worked to make the new robot. Finally he finished. It was time to try out the brand-new RoboMan. Would he be able to do the five things? Would the project be a success? The professor tried him out, and Yes! He could do all five of the things he was created to do. RoboMan was a success!

Ask your child, Why was RoboMan a success? *If need be, lead him or her to the answer:* It was a success because RoboMan did what he was created to do. The robot fulfilled the purpose Professor Gizmo created him for.

Human beings are successful when we fulfill the purpose for which God created us. When we do the things God wants us to do, we are a success in His eyes. God created us to obey His Word and follow His guidance throughout life. When we do that, we are a success!

Do you want to be a success?

Biblical Principles of Success

Teaching your children what God has to say about success will go a long way toward molding their outlook on success in adulthood. Here are some key points you will want to make:

- *Only hard workers are successful* (Proverbs 24:30-34). (Review "Good Work Habits" under "Building a Virtuous Heart.")

- *Always put God first in your life.* God must come before your self-interests, your career, your family, and, indeed, before everything (Matthew 6:33,34). Then God will bless your efforts.

- *Be wholehearted in your commitment to God.* Don't be like Amaziah, who "did what was right in the eyes of the Lord, but not wholeheartedly" (2 Chronicles 25:2).

- *Always seek to remain in the center of God's will.* Try to imitate godly men like Hezekiah: "In everything that he undertook in the service of God's temple and in obedience to the law and the commands, he sought his God and worked wholeheartedly. And so he prospered" (2 Chronicles 31:21).

- *Always remain faithful to God in all things, and He will prosper you.* The words of Joshua are a great summary of this principle:

> Be strong and very courageous. Be careful to obey all the law my servant Moses gave you; do not turn from it to the right or to the left, that you may be successful wherever you go. Do not let this Book of the Law depart from your mouth; meditate on it day and night, so that you may be careful to do everything written in it. Then you will be prosperous and successful. Have I not commanded you? Be strong and courageous. Do not be terrified; do not be discouraged, for the Lord your God will be with you wherever you go (Joshua 1:7-9).

By following principles such as these, we will enjoy success God's way.

2

Controlling Emotions

"Emotions should be servants, not
masters—or at least not tyrants."[1]
—*Robert Benson*

Three men were walking on a wall—
   Feeling, Faith, and Fact.
When Feeling got an awful fall,
   Then Faith was taken back.
So close was Faith to Feeling,
   That he stumbled and fell too.
But Fact remained and pulled Faith back,
   And Faith brought Feeling too.[2]

Because uncontrolled emotions can pull one's faith down
and wreak havoc in one's life, it is critically important that
we help our children come to grips with their emotions and
keep them in proper perspective. This can be a daunting task,
and it can take a long time. But with consistent effort, you
will see positive results.

Solomon provides us with numerous gems of insight regarding the types of things that give rise to different kinds
of emotions. Talk to your child about some of these points.

- Those who make a habit of living in righteousness typically enjoy a life characterized by joy and gladness
  (Proverbs 10:28; 29:6).

- Those who promote peace have joy in their lives (Proverbs 12:20).

- A key to contentment is maintaining a continual reverence for God (Proverbs 19:23).

- Jealousy can virtually consume a person and, if unchecked, can lead him or her to get out of control (Proverbs 6:34,35; 27:4).

As you share these insights with your child, try to provide real-life examples that illustrate them.

Learning Self-Control

Instead of being controlled *by* our feelings, God wants us to learn self-control *over* them.

"A fool gives full vent to his anger, but a wise man keeps himself under control" (Proverbs 29:11).

As we read through the book of Proverbs, we get the distinct feeling that Solomon has personally experienced agonizing depressions as well as ecstatic joys in his life. Through it all, God imparted tremendous wisdom to him regarding the emotional makeup of man. Solomon sought to pass this wisdom on to his "son." His goal was to ensure that this son would learn that insofar as emotions are concerned, wisdom urges self-control.

Sharing Time: Your Emotional Temperature

Sheryl Bruinsma has come up with a great way of talking to a child about self-control over emotions. (Have a thermometer on hand for this illustration.)

Can you tell me what this is? It takes your temperature. It is called a thermometer. When would your mother or a doctor use a thermometer with you? When they think you are sick.

If your temperature is too high, you have a fever. How can this thermometer tell if you have a fever? There are numbers on the side that say what your temperature is. Do you know what your body temperature should be? About 98.6 is normal. . . . If you have a fever, you might run a slight temperature of 99 or 100. If it gets to 101, 102, or 103, it gets more serious, and something needs to be done about it. If it gets over 104, it is very serious. You are very sick.

You have an emotional temperature, also. Emotions are your feelings. If you are feeling calm and happy, you do not have an emotional fever. You might get a slight case of irritation or get mad about something for a minute or two and then it goes away. You might cry about something and then it is all right again. That happens.

If, however, you get very angry, and your emotional temperature continues to build, that's not good. You don't want to let your emotional temperature climb and climb. You need to do something to get it lowered. You need to talk about what's making you feel bad. You need to solve the problem. You need to get your feelings under control.

If you let your emotions get hotter and hotter, you might explode into action and do or say something you will regret. Just like a fever of 104 or more, an emotional fever is dangerous.[3]

Getting a Grip on Anger

Unmanaged anger can ruin a child's life and the lives of those around him. The challenge for parents is to teach their children to manage their anger. If parents fail here, their children are truly headed for a life of hurts.

God desires that each of us learn to handle and express anger in appropriate ways.

" 'In your anger do not sin': Do not let the sun go down while you are still angry" (Ephesians 4:26).

Everyone gets mad, and many express their anger inappropriately. These expressions include:

- attacking with hands, feet, and weapons (sticks, toys, and so forth)

- becoming verbally abusive, such as screaming and using expletives

- throwing a tantrum and/or damaging property

- becoming highly self-critical for failing to maintain control

- withdrawing from those who caused the anger and not dealing with the emotion at all

- turning the anger inward where it will turn to bitter resentment.

Lowering the Emotional Temperature in Your Home

If your children are having difficulty with anger, it may be that your household needs to have its emotional temperature lowered. We must begin with ourselves. It is important that we, as parents, model the correct way to respond to anger for our children. They learn how to deal with their emotions by watching and imitating how mom and dad handle theirs. If your kids are having a lot of problems with emotions, well, you might want to do a self-examination to make sure you're okay in this area. In doing a self-examination, Dr. Ross Campbell suggests that you ask yourself nine questions:

1. Do I vent my anger in a mature, responsible way?

2. Am I usually optimistic?

3. Do I complain about those in authority over me at church or work?

4. Do I show respect for my child's other parent?

5. Do I want my children to develop character like mine?

6. Do I go off on tirades?

7. Do I forgive others easily?

8. Do I ask my children to forgive me when I'm wrong?

9. Are my children afraid to approach me because I might blow up?[4]

By asking yourself these kinds of questions, you can recognize blind spots in your character. Correct these and you may witness your child's anger decreasing.

There are three further points that bear mentioning:

1. Teach your children simple coping techniques such as taking a deep breath and counting to ten. Some cooldown time spent in one's room can also be extremely beneficial as a means of avoiding rash actions or words.

2. Allow and encourage your children to verbally express their anger in a calm way. Children must be allowed to express *why* they feel the way they do, even if it involves pointing a finger toward you (and, yes, there will be occasions when they're right about something you did wrong). If allowed to give *verbal* expression, kids will be less likely to give *physical* expression to their anger.

   Of course, you must be careful not to allow your child to cross the boundary into disrespect. Verbal expressions are allowed, but verbal assaults are off-limits.

3. Keep the lines of communication open and talk a lot. Your children need to know that mom and dad are always there with an open ear. If they feel like you never listen, their anger temperature will definitely rise.

3

Handling Failure

"If at first you don't succeed, relax; you're just like the rest of us."

—*Anonymous*

Most children have heard of Abraham Lincoln. Lincoln once said, "I do the very best I know how—the very best I can; and I mean to keep doing so." Despite the fact that Lincoln consistently tried to do his best, he experienced many failures. Consider this brief chronology of Lincoln's career:[1]

1832—Defeated for legislature
1838—Defeated for speaker
1840—Defeated for elector
1848—Defeated for congress
1855—Defeated for senate
1856—Defeated for vice-president
1858—Defeated for senate
1860—Elected president

Lincoln had a lot of failures before he had any success. Even the people we like to think of as being most successful have often had plenty of failures in their lives. It's important for kids to understand this, because sometimes, with their limited perspective, they get the feeling that *only they* fail at things. But failure is common to all humanity.

We need to allow our children the freedom to fail. They should have the space to have ups and downs in their lives. It is in their failures that they will learn the most. As pastor Erwin Lutzer once put it, "Often the doorway to success is entered through the hallway of failure."[2]

Jesus allowed His disciples the freedom to fail. In each case, the failing disciple learned an important lesson. For instance, Jesus allowed Peter to sink into the water so he would learn to keep his eyes on Christ (Matthew 14:28-31). He also allowed the disciples to fail in casting out a demon so they would learn the weakness of their own flesh (Matthew 17:14-21).[3]

In allowing our children the freedom to experience failure, they learn what works and what doesn't work in life. This is so valuable for them!

 We can learn from our failures.

"Let us not become weary in doing good, for at the proper time we will reap a harvest if we do not give up" (Galatians 6:9).

Did you know that Thomas Edison was once mocked for unsuccessfully trying 5,000 different materials for the filament of the lightbulb he was trying to invent? Someone told him, "You failed 5,000 times." Edison quickly countered, "I have not failed. I have discovered 5,000 materials that won't work."[4] Edison learned from his experiences and moved on to success.

Sharing Time: They Became Successful!

Did You Know—

• Willie Mays struck out his first 29 times at bat before he became one of the greatest major league batters of all time?

- Jim Abbott was born with only one hand, but he pitched the victorious gold medal game for the United States Olympic team?

- Michael Jordan was cut from his ninth-grade basketball team because he wasn't good enough? He later became one of the greatest basketball players in the world.

- Warren Moon's junior-high coach said he stunk as a quarterback, but later he became one of the greatest quarterbacks ever?

- Joe Montana was knocked out of the game "permanently" before he led the 49ers to a Super Bowl championship?[5]

In each case, the individual learned something from his failure and went on to become a success. So, the next time you fail, remember that failure can be a learning experience that can eventually lead you to success.

Of course, we shouldn't just let our children experience failure and leave it at that. We need to teach them appropriate ways of handling failure. We need to model for them appropriate responses for them.

In an office building, I once saw one of those huge screens on which a "message for the day" was flashed. On that particular day the message was, "If at first you don't succeed, destroy all evidence that you ever tried." That's not a healthy attitude. As we noted, some of our greatest victories will come out of our failures—as was true with the famous personalities that were just listed.

What, then, should we teach our kids about failure? Here are four suggestions.

1. *Teach your children that they are not failures.* If they fail at a particular task, that doesn't mean that they (as persons) are failures. You might mention a failure in your own life to illustrate this fact.

2. *Point your children to God, who is with us in all our failures*
   (Psalm 34:19,20). God is an ever-present help in time of
   need. Emphasize that Christ's strength kicks into high
   gear in our lives when we sense our own weakness (2
   Corinthians 12:9).

3. *Teach your children that God gives us a new beginning every
   day.* Point out how some of the biblical saints failed.
   Peter, for example, denied Christ three times. That's a
   pretty major failure. But he recovered and got his life
   back on track. Just because he failed didn't mean his life
   was over. We have new mercies from God every morning
   (Lamentations 3:22,23). That's a great truth for us to remember.

4. *Teach your children to interpret failures as learning experiences.* Help them see that we learn what to do in the present and future by mistakes made in the past. We are in
   the school of life. As Charles Swindoll put it, "Great accomplishments are often attempted but only occasionally reached. Those who reach them are usually those
   who missed many times before. Failures are only temporary tests to prepare us for permanent triumphs."[6]

4

Making Wise Decisions

"The mind grows by what it feeds on." [1]
—Josiah Holland

A frightened fifth-grader stood silently before his father, who was sternly reviewing an unsatisfactory report card. Grasping at anything to break the deafening silence, the youngster said, "Do you think those grades are the result of heredity or could it just be my environment?"

Like every student in a jam, this boy was looking for an excuse. The father was not amused. But the lad had a point. [2]

Scripture says God created human beings in His image. Part of that image involves a rational nature. It follows then that we must teach our children to use their God-given capacity to reason for the glory of God.

We need to help our children learn to think and make decisions for themselves. If you make all decisions for them in their childhood, they won't be prepared to make any decisions when they leave home. We mustn't be so overprotective that they are shielded from real life. We should allow them to make as many age-appropriate decisions as they can.

 God wants us to *train* our minds so we can make the right decisions in life.

"Test everything. Hold on to the good" (1 Thessalonians 5:21).

God gave us minds so that we can think. Our minds need to be trained so we can make the best decisions. The following are a few training exercises to help your children learn to make the best decisions:

- When you give your kids an allowance, help them think through alternatives on the best way to spend—or save— it! Let them make the final decision, but walk them through all their options. This will help them learn to weigh alternatives.

- As you and your spouse make important decisions, you don't necessarily have to go through the process out of sight of your children. If appropriate, let your children witness you wrestling through the choices. In so doing, they will pick up decision-making skills as they see how you discussed alternatives.[3]

- Help your children start thinking in terms of taking the long look. Help them see that present decisions can have an effect on the future. An example would be the fact that if a child commits to saving his allowance instead of spending it today, a few months from now he can buy that costly toy he's been wanting for so long.

Guarding the Mind

We make better decisions if we fill our minds with good things.

> *"Finally, brothers, whatever is true, whatever is noble, whatever is right, whatever is pure, whatever is lovely, whatever is admirable—if anything is excellent or praiseworthy—think about such things"* (Philippians 4:8).

There's an old saying: "Garbage in; garbage out." If we fill our minds with garbage, then garbage will come out of our minds. If kids are always watching violent TV shows, then their minds will have more violent thoughts, and those thoughts may translate into violence on the playground. If your kids hang around others who use unacceptable language, then unacceptable language may start coming out of their mouths.

Sharing Time: A Bandage For the Heart

Sheryl Bruinsma has a great way of illustrating the importance of filling our minds with good thoughts:

> Is there anyone here who has never needed a bandage? We all need one at one time or another. Why? What does a bandage do? It protects our cuts and sores. First you clean out a cut. You might need to apply pressure to get it to stop bleeding. Then you put on a bandage to keep the germs out. It is important to keep the germs out so your cut does not become infected.
>
> When the Bible tells us to think about things that are good and honest and beautiful, it is telling us to keep out the bad germs that might infect us. Let's think of some bad germs that might get inside our minds and hearts. How about hating? If you hate someone, you dislike her so much that you are mean to her. If you hate someone, you feel mean inside. This meanness can infect you so that you become mean to other people, and you feel miserable. Jealousy is another bad germ. If you are jealous of your friend, you want what he has. You become infected with wanting, and you do not appreciate what you have. You become unhappy. Lying is another bad germ. One lie leads to another until you have an infection of lies.
>
> How do you keep these and other bad germs out? What kind of bandage can you put on your heart? The Bible tells us to keep a bandage of pure, clean thoughts on our hearts. If we cover our hearts with good thoughts, it will be very hard for the bad germs to get in. If you love people with Jesus' love, it will be hard to begin to hate. You will forgive someone long before you can start hating her. If you thank God for your blessings and enjoy all the wonderful things He has given you, you

won't have time for jealousy. If you value truth and are honest, the lies won't creep in.

Keep the germs out of your heart and mind. Protect yourself with good thoughts.[4]

Using the Bible to Gain Guidance

In making major decisions, it is always wise to seek guidance from the Word of God.

"Your word is a lamp to my feet and a light for my path" (Psalm 119:105).

Susan Yates, who often writes on child-related issues, suggests showing kids how to use a "filter" in making decisions. She says that the filter on her coffeepot strains out the grounds and leaves a pure, delicious cup of coffee. Kids need a filter to help them sort through their thoughts while making decisions.

> The most important filter your child can have in any decision-making process is the Word of God. God speaks directly to certain issues—and makes it clear that such things as lying and having sex outside of marriage are wrong. Teach your children to refer to the Bible when faced with decision-making by setting the example of doing the same when you deal with other people in your church, neighborhood, or workplace.[5]

Sharing Time: Lighting the Way

Back in biblical times, they didn't have streetlamps like we have today. They didn't have electricity or lightbulbs. So do you know what they did?

They made little clay pots specially designed to sit on top of a person's foot. The pots were filled with a little oil, and a wick was put in. It was lit just like a candle. It was a lamp on a foot. This way, when it was night, people who were walking outside could see where they were going. It's kind of like having a nightlight, isn't it?

The Bible is like that little lamp. Psalm 119:105 says, "Your word is a lamp to my feet and a light for my path." God's Word—the Bible—helps us to see where we should go in life.[6]

Of course, our kids will inevitably encounter certain issues that do not have black and white answers from the Bible. Teach them that when they confront such problems, they can draw principles from Scripture that will help them. For example, the two greatest commandments, "love God" and "love your neighbor," can often help us in making decisions.

Here's another consideration: The more we understand God's Word, the better our minds will be trained to recognized counterfeit belief systems. It's much like bankers who are trained to recognize counterfeit dollar bills. They spend a lot of time with real dollar bills, examining every quality, so that when a counterfeit shows up, they'll recognize it instantly.

Scripture says that "solid food [God's Word] is for the mature, who by constant use have trained themselves to distinguish good from evil" (Hebrews 5:14). As our minds are trained by Scripture, we are better equipped to recognize error and evil. Therefore it is wise to start our children in early childhood feeding upon God's Word for wisdom.

Seeking Godly Counsel

Before making big decisions, it is wise to seek advice from the people you trust.

"Many advisers make victory sure" (Proverbs 11:14).

One of the things we learn in the book of Proverbs is that it is wise to seek godly counsel before making major decisions, and when we are unsure about a course of action. A wise man seeks the wisdom of others.

Sharing Time: Joe's Two Cabins

Once upon a time, there was a man named Joe who decided to build a log cabin on a small mountain. He did the best he could—but everything went wrong. He built the windows crooked. The doors wouldn't stay shut. The roof wouldn't keep the rain out. It was terrible.

Joe decided to tear the cabin down and start all over. This time, though, he decided to get some advice. He asked a neighbor with a nice cabin how to build a good cabin. And the man in the cabin gave him lots of good advice on all the things to do to build a good cabin.

So Joe made another cabin—and this one turned out great! Like the Bible says, there is great wisdom in seeking advice from others.

5

Speaking in a God-Honoring Way

"Confine your tongue, lest it confine you."[1]

—*Anonymous*

The tongue can be used to bring great blessings to people. It can also do great damage. Our goal as parents should be to train our children to increasingly use their tongue to the glory of God.

 Speak words that bless and build up!

"Do not let any unwholesome talk come out of your mouths, but only what is helpful for building others up according to their needs, that it may benefit those who listen" (Ephesians 4:29).

According to Ephesians 4:29, our words should do two things: build people up, and benefit people in some way. If our words tear people down or harm them, they're doing the exact opposite of what God wants.

Sharing Time: A Mind Full of Weeds?

One of the ways to make sure that good things come out of our mouths is to make sure that only good things are going into our minds.

Suppose I put a bunch of chocolate cookies in a cookie jar. Then you come down the stairs and stick your hand into the cookie jar. What will you pull out? Cookies, of course!

Well, what if the next week I put weeds from our lawn into the cookie jar. Then you came down the stairs and put your hand into the cookie jar. What would you pull out? Weeds, of course! Whatever we put into the cookie jar is what we will pull out of the cookie jar.

The same thing is true of our lives. If we constantly put bad things into our minds—like listening to kids on the playground saying bad things, or maybe watching a TV show we shouldn't watch—we'll probably have some bad things come out of our mouths. But if we put good things into our minds, good things will come out.

Do you want to be like the cookie jar with cookies or like the cookie jar with weeds in it?[2]

Parental Models

In teaching our children to speak in a God-honoring way, the place to begin is to model this behavior for them. If we are abusive in the way we speak as parents, how can we expect our children not to do likewise?

Ask yourself if you do any of the following in front of your children:

- criticize people
- mock or ridicule people
- say unkind things about people
- tell "white lies"
- speak with a sarcastic or derisive tone of voice

Our children learn by observing us. If you want to teach your child how to speak rightly, be sure to start with yourself!

Learning to Guard Your Mouth

By guarding the things we say, we can keep ourselves out of a great deal of trouble.

"He who guards his mouth and his tongue keeps himself from calamity" (Proverbs 21:23).

Solomon, the wisest man who ever lived, often spoke of the importance of guarding the things we say. Consider:

- "He who guards his lips guards his life, but he who speaks rashly will come to ruin" (Proverbs 13:3).

- "An evil man is trapped by his sinful talk, but a righteous man escapes trouble" (Proverbs 12:13).

- "A fool's talk brings a rod to his back, but the lips of the wise protect them" (Proverbs 14:3).

Do you want to be as wise as Solomon? One way to imitate him is to watch what you say!

Sharing Time: Words and Feathers

The story is told of a young man during the Middle Ages who went to a wise man, saying, "I've sinned by saying some bad things about someone. What can I do to take back what I said and undo the damage of my words?"

The wise man replied, "Put a feather on every doorstep in town."

The young man did it. He then returned to the wise man, wondering if there was anything else he should do.

The wise man said, "Go back and pick up all the feathers."

The young man replied, "That's impossible! By now the wind will have blown them all over town!"

Said the wise man, "So have your slanderous words become impossible to retrieve."[3]

It is better to *think* before speaking because once we've hurt someone with our words it's hard to undo the damage. We should put a "guard" at our mouth to make sure nothing bad escapes from it.

The Tongue Is Like . . .

The tongue wields tremendous power and must therefore be controlled.

"When we put bits into the mouths of horses to make them obey us, we can turn the whole animal" (James 3:3).

"Take ships as an example. Although they are so large and are driven by strong winds, they are steered by a very small rudder wherever the pilot wants to go. Likewise the tongue is a small part of the body, but it makes great boasts" (James 3:4,5).

"Consider what a great forest is set on fire by a small spark. The tongue also is a fire, a world of evil among the parts of the body. It corrupts the whole person, sets the whole course of his life on fire, and is itself set on fire by hell" (James 3:5,6).

What do we learn from these verses? The tongue is small but influential. The tongue is petite but powerful.

- A bridle bit is small but it wields tremendous influence over a horse.

- A rudder is small yet it determines in which direction the ship goes.

- A small spark can set a whole forest on fire.

In the same way, the tongue is a small organ but it can have a powerful influence—for good or bad.

Sharing Time: Putting the Squeeze on Words

It will help to have a tube of toothpaste for this illustration.

Pretend that you are a tube of toothpaste. Every time you speak a word, that's like a little toothpaste coming out of the tube. When you say a lot of words, that's a lot of toothpaste coming out of the tube. Whether you say nice words or hurtful words, it's like toothpaste coming out of the tube.

Now, let's pretend that you say some hurtful words to someone. (Squeeze the tube so some toothpaste comes out.) Later you're sorry and wish you hadn't said those bad words. But can we take those words back? Can we put the toothpaste back into the tube?

No, we can't. Once the toothpaste comes out of the tube, it's out forever. And that's the way our words are. Once we speak them, they're out for good. The damage is done.

That's why it's so important to watch what we say before we say it. The tongue is small, but it must be controlled. If we don't control it, it does damage that we can't undo.[4]

6

Gaining a Healthy
Self-Concept

"A healthy self-image is seeing yourself
as God sees you—no more and no less."[1]
—*Josh McDowell*

During a sermon, one of my seminary friends spoke about how some people feel a need to cover up a lack of self-confidence by trying to make a big impression. He told the story of a newly promoted army colonel who moved into his new and impressive office. As he sat behind his big desk, a private knocked at his door. "Just a minute," the colonel said, "I'm on the phone."

He picked up the phone and said loudly, "Yes, sir, General, I'll call the president this afternoon. No, sir, I won't forget." Then he hung up the phone and told the private to come in.

"What can I help you with?" the colonel asked.

"Well, sir," the private replied, "I've come to hook up your phone."

All of us want other people to like us and be impressed with us. Our children are no exception. Sometimes kids look in the mirror and are tempted to say, "Thanks a lot, God. You really blew it when you made me." Some kids think they're too fat, too thin, too tall, have a big nose, have a funny voice, bowed legs, big feet, acne, big ears, crooked teeth, no muscles, no talents, not enough brains, and much more (or much worse).

Today, all of us are tempted to focus on external appearances. Just look at the ads on TV. Many of the products we see advertised are supposed to help us look younger or better in some way. We're conditioned to think that we do not look good enough just as we are.

Scripture tells us that while man may look on external appearances, God looks on the heart (1 Samuel 16:7). *It is crucial to instill this wisdom in our children.* We need to help them see the importance of inner beauty, which is lasting, as opposed to outer beauty, which fades quickly.

 God looks not on external appearances but on the heart.

"The LORD does not look at the things man looks at. Man looks at the outward appearance, but the LORD looks at the heart" (1 Samuel 16:7).

What Are You Modeling?

In teaching our children the truth of 1 Samuel 16:7, the place to begin is with ourselves. What do our children see us modeling? Do we subtly communicate to them that people absolutely have to have those advertised beauty "extras" in order to appear right? Or do we communicate the importance of inner beauty? Our children are watching. They pick up on our attitudes and imitate them.[2] Are you excessively preoccupied with your appearance? If so, you are teaching your child to do the same.[3]

Also ask yourself, Do my verbal compliments to my children regarding dress, hair, and outward appearance outnumber my compliments on their character, efforts, and jobs well done? If the answer is yes, then make it a point to correct the ratio, remembering that inward beauty is more worthy of compliment.

Sharing Time: God Sees Our Hearts

You've seen peanuts, haven't you? Sure you have!

Peanuts don't look that great on the outside, do they? In fact, the shells of the peanuts look kind of old and rough. They're kind of lumpy, and they're shaped funny.

But when you open up that shell, you find a beautiful, delicious peanut inside. *Yum.* It tastes great; and it looks great. It's odd that something so nice would be inside something that doesn't look so great. But that's the way God made peanuts. I love peanuts, even though they don't look that great on the outside.

That's kind of the way it is with people, too. Now, I think you look great on the outside. But the important thing is not what we look like on the outside, but what we're like on the inside. God looks at our hearts, not at our hairstyle or our clothes.[4]

Fearfully and Wonderfully Made

In Psalm 139:13,14 the psalmist affirmed to God, "For you created my inmost being; you knit me together in my mother's womb. I praise you because I am fearfully and wonderfully made; your works are wonderful, I know that full well."

We are fearfully and wonderfully made! God made us just the way we are. Despite this, our kids are still very sensitive about the way they look. So here's a piece of advice. You will be a forever friend with your child if you make special efforts to do what you can to enhance his or her natural beauty. Now, I'm not contradicting what I said earlier. I'm not saying we should communicate that they need all those beauty extras to be attractive. What *I am* saying is:

- take them to a dermatologist if they're breaking out with acne
- take them to an orthodontist if their teeth are crooked
- let them get their hair styled
- provide appropriate and fashionable clothing

I guarantee your child will appreciate all this!

A Point Made from Biblical History

A look at biblical history reveals that many of the people who made the greatest impact on this world have not exactly been physical specimens of beauty. Consider John the Baptist. Scripture tells us that "John's clothes were made of camel's hair, and he had a leather belt round his waist. His food was locusts and wild honey" (Matthew 3:4).

Despite this apparent unattractiveness (according to the world's standards), Jesus said of John the Baptist, "Among those born of women there has not risen anyone greater than John the Baptist" (Matthew 11:11). That's high praise!

And consider Jesus Christ. Very often we see paintings of Jesus that portray a very good-looking man—sort of like a model with long hair. Yet Isaiah, the prophet, said of Jesus, "He had no beauty or majesty to attract us to him, nothing in his appearance that we should desire him" (Isaiah 53:2).

This brings us back to the main point: God is more concerned about inner beauty than outer beauty.

Now, it is interesting that the Bible talks not only about individuals with little external beauty that were mightily used of God (such as John the Baptist), but also talks about those with tremendous beauty who ended upon sinning woefully against God. Saul is an example. We read in 1 Samuel 9:2 that Saul was "an impressive young man without equal among the Israelites—a head taller than any of the others." Physically he was hard to beat. He looked good. He was chosen to be Israel's king. But Saul sinned against God and rejected God's Word—and the Lord rejected him as king (see 1 Samuel 15:22,23).

The moral of the story is: *What you look like on the outside ultimately means very little. What you're like on the inside means a great deal.*

7

Dealing with Peers

"He who lies down with dogs shall rise up with fleas."

—*Benjamin Franklin*

A farmer, troubled by a flock of crows in his cornfield, loaded his shotgun. He crawled unseen along the fence-row, determined to get a shot at the crows.

Now, the farmer had a very "sociable" parrot who made friends with everybody. Seeing the flock of crows, the parrot flew over and joined them (just being sociable, you know).

The farmer saw the crows but didn't see the parrot. He took careful aim and bang!

The farmer crawled over the fence to pick up the fallen crows, and lo, there was his parrot badly ruffled, with a broken wing, but still alive. Tenderly, the farmer carried the parrot home, where his children met him.

Seeing that their pet was injured, they tearfully asked, "What happened, Papa?"

Before he could answer, the parrot spoke up: "Bad company!"[1]

Scripture warns us to be careful about who we hang around with because bad company can have a bad influence on us. This is a crucial lesson for our children to learn.

Peer Influence

Choose your friends carefully.

"Bad company corrupts good character" (1 Corinthians 15:33).

"He who walks with the wise grows wise, but a companion of fools suffers harm" (Proverbs 13:20).

God's Word reminds us that children tend to become more and more like their frequent companions. Indeed, as Norman Bull put it, "the nature of a child's morality will depend upon those around him—upon, that is, the identifications he makes."[2]

Make no mistake about it. Your children's friends *will* influence their behavior. And they will seek to avoid rejection or humiliation in front of their peers at all costs. This concern for peers will, in the future, motivate your children to do things you'd never think they'd even consider. For this reason, as much as possible, it is important that you as a parent steer your children toward the kinds of friendships that will be healthy for them.

Sharing Time: Walk Away!

Steve, Frank, and Gary were good friends. One day Steve and Frank asked Gary to come with them to a construction site on a weekend. A new house was being built, and none of the workmen were there that day.

The site was marked with a no trespassing sign. Right then and there, Gary knew that it was not a wise thing to do. He went along anyway. They went inside the house to explore. There were lots of tools laying around. There were some nails on the floor, too.

Steve and Frank decided they wanted to break a few windows with a hammer. Gary didn't want to do this, but they teased him. They called him a chicken. They said they'd tell the other guys at school that Gary was a chicken. So, Gary joined Steve and Frank in breaking some windows.

They didn't plan on getting caught. But a neighbor across the street saw what they did and called their parents.

Gary's dad asked him, "How do you think it makes your mom and I feel that you did this? And how do you think the Lord feels about what you did?"

Gary answered, "I guess it makes all of you feel sad. I'm sorry for doing it. I shouldn't have listened to Steve and Frank."

Gary had to pay for his share of the broken windows with his allowance. He learned a good lesson that day. He should have walked away while the walking was good. God wants us to always do right, even when our friends try to make us do wrong.

Solomon on Friendship

Solomon, the author of the book of Proverbs, has a lot to say about friendship. Although he was a famous and rich man, he still needed friends to whom he could turn for companionship. Someone once said that friendship is the universal need among all people—whether rich or poor, male or female, black or white. God made humans with a built-in need for companionship.

The book of Proverbs provides us with rich insights for making our friendships as fulfilling and meaningful as possible within the confines of a fallen world. As a teaching tool, you might ask your child why he or she thinks Solomon said what he did in each of the Proverbs below.

People to Avoid:

Proverbs 22:24: "Do not make friends with a hot-tempered man, do not associate with one easily angered."

Question: Why do you think Solomon said not to make friends with hot-tempered people?

Proverbs 20:19: "A gossip betrays a confidence; so avoid a man who talks too much."

Question: Why do you think Solomon said to keep your distance from people who gossip too much?

Proverbs 26:18,19: "Like a madman shooting firebrands or deadly arrows is a man who deceives his neighbor and says, 'I was only joking!' "

Question: Why do you think Solomon said not to befriend people who are dishonest?

Proverbs 13:10: "Pride only breeds quarrels but wisdom is found in those who take advice."

Question: Why do you think Solomon said not to make friends with people who have too much pride or think too highly of themselves?

People to Seek Out:

Proverbs 2:20; 12:26: "Thus you will walk in the ways of good men and keep to the paths of the righteous. . . . A righteous man is cautious in friendship, but the way of the wicked leads them astray."

Question: Why do you think Solomon said to make friends with righteous people?

Proverbs 17:9: "He who covers over an offense promotes love, but whoever repeats the matter separates close friends."

Question: Why do you think Solomon said to make friends with people who show love in their words and actions?

Proverbs 20:3: "It is to a man's honor to avoid strife, but every fool is quick to quarrel."

Question: Why do you think Solomon said to make friends with people who don't fight and argue?

General Principles on Friendship:

Proverbs 25:17: "Seldom set foot in your neighbor's house—too much of you, and he will hate you."

Question: Why do you think Solomon said that no matter who you make friends with, don't overstay your welcome?

Proverbs 3:3,4: "Let love and faithfulness never leave you; bind them around your neck, write them on the tablet of your heart. Then you will win favor and a good name in the sight of God and man."
Question: Why do you think Solomon said to let love and faithfulness characterize all your friendships?

Proverbs 22:1: "A good name is more desirable than great riches; to be esteemed is better than silver or gold."
Question: Why do you think Solomon said to maintain a good reputation in all your relationships?

Monitoring Your Child's Relationships

It's in your child's best interest for you to monitor his or her relationships. How can you do this? Here are three quick suggestions:[3]

- First, make your house a fun place so your child's friends will want to come over and spend lots of time there. Make your home a hangout. This way you can monitor things. Have plenty of games and fun things around. Homemade chocolate chip cookies are always nice!

- Second, involve your child in a church youth group so he or she will meet some Christian friends with similar interests.

- Third, stay in contact with your child's teacher. Often your teacher can keep you informed not only in regard to the kinds of friends your child hangs around with, but she can also give you an understanding of your child's social interaction skills on the school campus.

No Compromise: Growing Strong in the Faith

1

God's Book—The Bible

"God the Father is the giver of Holy Scripture; God the Son is the theme of Holy Scripture; and God the Spirit is the author, authenticator, and interpreter of Holy Scripture."[1]

— *J.I. Packer*

The word "Bible" means book. The Bible is God's book for us. Much like a manufacturer's handbook, the Bible instructs us how to operate our lives. It's like an eyeglass. Without the eyeglass, we can't see clearly. We see only a blurred reality. But with the eyeglass, everything comes into clear focus. We see God as He really is. Like a lamp, the Bible sheds light on our paths and helps us see our way clearly. Psalm 119:105 says, "Your word is a lamp to my feet and a light for my path." And just as an anchor keeps a boat from floating away, so the Bible anchors us. It prevents us from being swept away when a tidal wave of adversity comes our way.

The Bible is also like food. It gives us spiritual nourishment. If we don't feed on God's Word, we become spiritually depleted. And the Bible is a love letter from God to us. It tells us about how God's great love for us motivated Him to send Jesus into the world to die for our sins so we could be saved.

Sharing Time: Our Valentine from God

On Valentine's Day we like to give people we love a Valentine card as a way of saying, "I love you." Mom and Dad always give Valentine cards to each other because we love each other. And we give a Valentine card to you because we love you, too!

Did you know that God has also given us a Valentine card? It's right here. It's the Bible. This book shows how much God loves each one of us.

The great thing is that we don't get this Valentine card from God just once a year on Valentine's Day. Instead, we have it to read every day. And as we read it, we are always reminded of God's love for us.

Of course, the most important way God shows us His love is that Jesus came and died for our sins. That's one of the most important things God's Valentine card teaches us![2]

God Speaks to Us Through the Bible

The Bible contains God's words to us.

"All Scripture is God-breathed and is useful for teaching, rebuking, correcting and training in righteousness" (2 Timothy 3:16).

God is the one who caused the Bible to be written. We should help our children understand that through the Bible God speaks to us just as He spoke to people in ancient times when those words were first given. The Bible is to be received as *God's words to us* and obeyed as such. As we submit to the Bible's authority, we place ourselves under the authority of the living God.

The Scriptures "are God preaching, God talking, God telling, God instructing, God setting before us the right way to think and speak about him. The Scriptures are God showing us himself: God communicating to us who he is and what he has done so that in the response of faith we may truly know him and live our lives in fellowship with Him."[3]

Sharing Time: The Owner's Manual

When I bought my car, it came with an owner's manual. Do you know what that is? It's a book that explains everything I need to know about how to make my car work. It tells me certain things I need to do—such as putting oil in the car so it will run smoothly. The manual also tells me certain things I should not do—such as driving the car without oil.

The people who made my car know just how it should be taken care of. As long as I follow their instructions, everything should work great on my car. But if I ignore the instructions—the owner's manual—then something might break on my car.

God is the one who made you and me. Do you know what our "owner's manual" is? It's the Bible. God, who made us, knows just how we should operate our lives. As long as we follow God's instructions, our lives will run smoothly. But if we ignore God's instructions, things go wrong.

Do you want to follow God's instructions?[4]

Scripture Is Inspired

It is amazing to contemplate that the Bible's authors were from all walks of life: kings, peasants, philosophers, fishermen, physicians, statesmen, scholars, poets, and farmers. These individuals lived in different cultures, had vastly different experiences, and often were quite different in character. Yet the Bible has a continuity from Genesis to Revelation.

How could this be? How did God accomplish this? It's related to a process we call inspiration.

Biblical inspiration may be defined as God's superintending of the human authors so that, using their own individual personalities and even their writing styles, they composed and recorded without error His revelation to man. Because of inspiration, we can rest assured that what the human authors wrote was precisely what God wanted written.

Sharing Time: God Was in Charge

Sometimes at school, classes put on plays. And every student in the class gets to be somebody in the play.

Do you know who stands backstage to make sure everyone says exactly the right words? It's the teacher. The teacher is always there to make sure everyone is saying everything just right. She's there to make sure no one makes any mistakes. She's the one in charge. And everyone listens to her directions.

Well, when men in biblical times were writing the books of the Bible, God made sure they wrote exactly the right words with no mistakes. He made sure that everything written in the Bible is exactly what He wanted to be written. He was in charge. Everyone listened to His instructions. From beginning to end, He made sure all the Bible books were just right.

How the Bible Books Came Together

After a Bible book was written in Old Testament times, it was carefully copied by Jewish scribes so it could be distributed to other people interested in reading it. In the New Testament, Jesus often quoted from these Old Testament books. He said they were all true (see Matthew 5:17-20).

Later, during New Testament times, other books of the Bible were written by people who had seen Jesus or had close contact with Him. The New Testament is based on eyewitness testimony.

Still later, in the early centuries of Christianity, a group of godly men got together and formally agreed with what God had already revealed—that 66 books written in the Old and New Testament times belong in the Bible. Ever since then, these 66 books have been bound together as a single book.

No One Can Add to the Bible Today

No one can add to or take anything away from the Bible. It is the finished and completed book of God.

"I warn everyone who hears the words of the prophecy of this book: If anyone adds anything to them, God will add to him the plagues described in this book. And if anyone takes words away from this book of prophecy, God will take away from him his share in the tree of life and in the holy city, which are described in this book" (Revelation 22:18,19).

It's very important for our children to understand that no one has the freedom to add new books to the Bible. God has already told us everything we need to know about Him and His will in the Bible; He is not going to give us any new Bibles (see Jude 3). This is important to learn, because there are some religious groups today, such as the Mormons and the Unification Church, who have tried to add to the Bible. The Bible is finished, from beginning to end. It will be our one and only book from God throughout our entire lives.

The Bible Is True

The things you read about in the Bible are true. None of it is make believe.

"We did not follow cleverly invented stories when we told you about the power and coming of our Lord

Jesus Christ, but we were eyewitnesses of his majesty" (2 Peter 1:16).

It's important for your child to understand that the stories in the Bible are not fairy tales. The Bible talks about *real* people and *real* events. God does not lie to us, and since the Bible is His book, we can depend on it. Even when the Bible talks about miracles, such as Jesus raising someone from the dead, we can trust it.

The Bible Is a Jesus Book

From beginning to end, the Bible is a book about Jesus.

"You diligently study the Scriptures because you think that by them you possess eternal life. These are the Scriptures that testify about me, yet you refuse to come to me to have life" (John 5:39,40).

"And beginning with Moses and all the Prophets, he explained to them what was said in all the Scriptures concerning himself" (Luke 24:27).

From beginning to end—from Genesis to Revelation—the Bible is about Jesus.

Many of the Jews to whom Jesus spoke knew the "shell" of the Bible but were neglecting the "kernel" within it. That is, they didn't recognize that Christ is the heart of Scripture. Jesus said the Scriptures were "concerning himself" (Luke 24:27), were "written about me" (verse 44), were "written of me" (Hebrews 10:7), and "testify about me" (John 5:39). You can best teach your child this truth by reading aloud selections from the four Gospels. (Mark is a fast-paced Gospel you might want to start with.)

Our Need to Read Scripture

We will grow spiritually if we read and meditate on Scripture.

"I delight in your decrees; I will not neglect your word" (Psalm 119:16).

In an interview, R.C. Sproul illustrated the importance of a time-commitment to Bible study with a story from his personal life:

> I have a friend who wants to learn how to play the piano. So I gave him a book of instructions that I put together over the years containing fifteen lessons. I sat down with him and said, "Now, if you will master these fifteen lessons, you're going to be off and running in your desire to play the piano."

Of course, his book contained just the basics. A person has to spend time mastering the fundamentals if he is really going to learn how to play the piano. Sproul said:

> My friend can gain great strides if he practices religiously for fifteen minutes a day. He'll definitely make some progress. But to understand the whole scope of music, he's never going to be an accomplished musician on fifteen minutes a day. No one's ever done that. Likewise, you can't be accomplished in your understanding of the riches of the things of God in five, or ten, or fifteen minutes a day.[5]

We should encourage our children to spend good time in the Scriptures. It is only by spending time with the Scriptures that they'll develop a love for God's Word.

Make Your Kids Hungry for the Bible

We should do all we can to help our kids become hungry for God's Word. Just as they feed on food to satisfy their hunger, so they need to feed on the Word of God to quench their spiritual thirst.

There are several things that can help you instill this thirst in your children.

1. First, you must model a thirst for God's Word in your own life. Your children will notice it if they consistently see you with a single book in your hands—the Bible. (They'll also notice if they never see that book in your hands.)[6]

2. Second, read the Bible with them. As you read, teach them to use the acrostic S-P-A-C-E:[7]

    S = *Sins* (Are there any sins in this verse I need to repent of?)

    P = *Promises* (Are there any promises in this verse I can claim?)

    A = *Attitudes* (Does this verse indicate I need an attitude change?)

    C = *Commands* (Are there any commands to obey in this verse?)

    E = *Example* (Is there an example to imitate in this verse?)

By using this acrostic, your children will learn to approach the Scriptures purposefully. By the time they're able to read on their own, this method of Bible study will have become part of the fabric of their lives.

Memorizing Bible Verses

Hide God's Word in your heart so you'll always have it with you!

"I have hidden your word in my heart that I might not sin against you" (Psalm 119:11).

"These commandments that I give you today are to be upon your hearts" (Deuteronomy 6:6).

We need to encourage our children to memorize God's Word. Hopefully your church is already helping in this area, but you should be involved in Scripture memory as a family, too. Remember—*you are a model.* Your children will imitate your behavior.

Have you ever seen a cactus? A cactus is a plant that is very prickly on the outside, but on the inside it stores a lot of water. This plant could not live without water. So whenever it rains, the cactus stores all the water it can. That's one reason the cactus plant lives for so long. And because the cactus stores up water inside, it can survive during long dry periods. It survives on what it has preserved inside.

I think God wants us to act like cactus plants. No, He doesn't want us to be prickly on the outside—but He does want us to store something inside us. He wants us to keep His Word in our hearts. He wants us to memorize Scripture so we'll always have it inside us.

Whenever you hear someone read the Bible—in church or at home—you should try to remember it and store it in your heart.[8]

It's often helpful to make Bible memorization a fun activity. There are many ways of doing this.[9] For example:

- If your child is old enough to write, get a chalkboard so he or she can write this week's verse on the board. Play games—such as writing the verse on the board with one or more words missing. Let your children figure out which words are missing.

- Have your children put each word from a verse on a separate index card. Then shuffle the cards and let your kids arrange the cards in the correct order.

- Let your children use a cassette recorder to practice reciting the verse aloud from memory.

- Involve the whole family by sitting in a circle and, going from one person to the next, reciting the verse word by word.

• There are many children's tapes that have verses set to music. They are great for memorizing Scripture for children and adults alike.

Sharing Time: Sponge Hearts

You might want to have a sponge and a bowl of water for this illustration.

Do you know what a sponge does? It soaks up water and liquids. God wants our hearts to be sponges that soak up His Word. The more we soak up God's Word, the closer we will be to God. Soaking up God's Word makes us healthy spiritually.[10]

Is your heart a sponge for God's Word?

2

Getting to Know God

"You are awesome, O God."[1]
—*King David*

One day after work, I walked into the living room and heard my daughter Kylie singing along with a praise tape. As I continued to listen, I discovered that she was singing praises to the Father, the Son, and the Holy Goat.

"Honey," I said, "let's have a little talk." And after our little talk, we had her concept of God all straightened out, and she's being singing praises to the true God ever since!

 There is only one true God.

"I am God, and there is no other; I am God, and there is none like me" (Isaiah 46:9).

There is one God and *only* one God. The true God has no rival. This is an especially important truth for our children to learn in view of the fact that New Agers say everything is God (including human beings), and Mormons say everyone has the potential to become a god.

Sharing Time: Only One You, Only One God

You may wish to lead your child through the following question-and-answer exercise to bring clearer understanding to the fact that God is the one and only true God.

How many you's are there? (*One.*)

Is there anyone else who is you? (*No.*)

If someone walked in the door right now and said they were you, would they really be the true you? (*No.*)

That's right! Because you are the *one and only* you. Nobody could ever be you but you.

That's how it is with God, as well. There is only one true God; there is only one God who is *really* God.

Now, back to you . . . We could stand you up next to someone who looked very much like you and who even had your name. We could say, "Wow, those two are a lot alike!" Would that mean there was another you? Of course not! *There is only one you.*

In God's case, He tells us that there is none like Him. No one and no thing could even come close to being like God. He can be compared to no one. He is the one and only true God.

Where Did God Come From?

Kids may sometimes wonder who created God. They may wonder who His parents are. Though it will be hard for them to grasp, teach your children that God was never born; He has never ceased to exist. He has always been there; He always *will* be there. God has no beginning or end.

This goes against all our experiences. After all, everything seems to have a beginning and an end. TV shows have a beginning and an end. Football games have a beginning and an end. Our pets have a beginning and an end (birth and death). Our loved ones have a beginning and an end. *But God had no birth, and He will never die.* He is eternal.

A good verse to teach your child is Psalm 90:1,2:

> Lord, you have been our dwelling place throughout all generations. Before the mountains were born or you

brought forth the earth and the world, from everlasting to everlasting you are God.

God Is Spirit

Children may occasionally ask you what God looks like. It is natural for them to wonder about this. Help them understand that God is invisible because He is a spirit and doesn't have a physical body like we do.

God is invisible because He is a spirit.

"God is spirit, and his worshipers must worship in spirit and in truth" (John 4:24).

The Scriptures inform us that God is Spirit. And a spirit does not have flesh and bones (Luke 24:39). Hence, it is wrong to think of God as a physical being. (At the same time, we need to keep in mind that when Jesus became a man in order to reveal God, He took on human flesh. So Jesus, from the moment He became a man, *did* have a physical body.)

Because God is a spirit, He is invisible (1 Timothy 1:17; John 1:18). Colossians 1:15 speaks of "the invisible God." But if God is a Spirit, then how are we to interpret the references in Scripture to God's face, ears, eyes, hands, strong arm, and the like (for example, see Exodus 33:11)? This is an important question.

The ancients often described God metaphorically in humanlike language because they considered Him very much alive and active in human affairs. To the men and women of the Old Testament, *God was real*. They knew Him as a person. And the clearest, most succinct way they could express their view of God and their interaction with Him was in the language of human personality and activity.

Such language, however, is not to be taken in a strict literal sense. When Moses spoke to God "face to face" (Exodus 33:11), this doesn't mean Moses saw a divine face with eyes, ears, a nose, and a mouth. Rather it means that Moses spoke to God *in His direct presence* and *in an intimate way.*

Sharing Time: Seeing God

When we buy a package of balloons at the store, we come home and then blow them up. That's fun to do.

We know that air is going into the balloon because the balloon is getting bigger and bigger. If we put too much air in the balloon, what happens? It pops.

Sometimes we blow air into the balloon and then let it out very slowly. As we let the air out, the balloon gets smaller and smaller, doesn't it?

We can't see the air, but we can sure see what the air does. Even though we can't see the air in the balloon, it makes the balloon get bigger or smaller if we let it out.

We can't see God either because He is invisible. But we can sure see the beautiful things God has made. God made the moon and all the stars in the sky. God made all the people in the world. God made all the animals. *God made you!*

Even though we don't see Him, God is always with us. He is invisible, but He is here.[2]

God Is a Trinity

There will inevitably come a time when you talk to your child about the Trinity. This is unquestionably one of the most difficult Bible doctrines to understand. I won't mince words here—this is a hard one. For us to be able to understand everything about God—including the doctrine of the Trinity—we'd have to have the very mind of God. Only a mind as great as God's could understand all there is to know about Him. Let me share a story involving the great theologian Augustine.

One day, while walking along the beach, Augustine was puzzling over the doctrine of the Trinity. On the beach he observed a young boy with a bucket, running back and forth to pour water into a little hole. Augustine asked, "What are you doing?"

The boy replied, "I'm trying to put the ocean into this hole."

Augustine smiled, recognizing the utter futility of what the boy was attempting to do.

After pondering the boy's words for a few moments, however, Augustine came to a sudden realization. He realized that he had been trying to put an infinite God into his finite mind. It can't be done.

We can accept God's revelation to us that He is triune in nature and that He has infinite perfections. But with our finite minds we cannot fully understand everything about God. *Our God is an awesome God!*

The doctrine of the Trinity states that there is only one God, but in the unity of the Godhead there are three co-equal and co-eternal persons: the Father, the Son, and the Holy Spirit. This doctrine is based on three lines of support in Scripture: 1) evidence that there is only one true God (Deuteronomy 6:4); 2) evidence that there are three persons who are God—the Father, Son, and Holy Spirit (1 Peter 1:2; John 20:28; Acts 5:3,4); and 3) evidence that indicates three-in-oneness within the Godhead (Matthew 28:19; 2 Corinthians 13:14).

There's no analogy that really does justice to the doctrine of the Trinity. But you might use the loose analogy of three-flavor ice cream.

Sharing Time: Three in One!

It would be helpful to have one container of ice cream that holds three flavors (Neapolitan).

Do you know what I have in this container? I have three flavors of ice cream! I have chocolate, vanilla, and strawberry ice cream. I have three separate flavors of ice cream in one carton.

Did you know that God is three in one, too? There is God the Father, God the Son, and God the Holy Spirit. Just like this ice cream has three flavors in one carton, so there are three persons in the one true God.

3

God and Man

God created you and me and everything else in the universe.

"God created man in his own image, in the image of God he created him; male and female he created them" (Genesis 1:27).

When God created the first man (Adam), He constructed him from the dust of the ground and breathed the breath of life into him (Genesis 2:7). How awesome a moment this must have been. At one moment no man existed; the next moment, there he stood. God then created Eve to be Adam's wife.

It is important for your children to understand that God created *all races* of people. We need to start very early to help our children have a biblical perspective of the races, so they will be prepared for the racism they will encounter in the world. All human beings are completely equal—including being equal in terms of their creation (Genesis 1:28), the sin problem (Romans 3:23), God's love for them (John 3:16), and God's provision of salvation for them (Matthew 28:19). The apostle Paul affirmed, "From one man he made every nation of men, that they should inhabit the whole earth; and he determined the times set for them and the exact places where they should live" (Acts 17:26).

Moreover, Revelation 5:9 tells us that God's redeemed will be from "every tribe and language and people and nation." There is no place for racial discrimination because all people are equal in God's sight.

Sharing Time: Painted by God

You might want to have crayons and M&Ms for this discussion.

God created all the people on this planet. And just like an artist likes to paint with all kinds of different colors, so God used different colors when He created people.

You like to use crayons, right? Think how boring it would be if all your crayons were just one color. It's much better to have crayons of many colors.

And what about M&Ms? You like M&Ms, right? Think how boring it would be if all your M&Ms were the same color, say yellow.

I like M&Ms. And I like the way all the different colors of M&Ms taste. They taste equally good, even though they're different colors.

In the same way, there are different colors of people on earth, and they're all equal in God's eyes. They should be equal in our eyes too.[1]

God Is Always Present with Us

 No matter where we are or where we go, God is always present with us.

"Where can I go from your Spirit? Where can I flee from your presence? If I go up to the heavens, you are there; if I make my bed in the depths, you are there" (Psalm 139:7,8).

How comforting to know that no matter where we go, we will never escape the presence of our beloved God. Because He is everywhere, we can be confident of His presence wherever we go. One way to teach your children is to talk about our senses:

It's true that we don't always perceive the presence of God but, nevertheless He's here with us. We should not be surprised that our physical senses are incapable of perceiving the spiritual presence of God. There are a lot of things we don't perceive. For instance, the deer of the forest has a very keen sense of smell, and smells odors we're not even aware of. The bat has a built-in radar system, enabling it to receive all kinds of information we don't perceive. Some animals of the forest have night vision, enabling them to see things that we can't without more light.

God is spiritually present with us. He is with us every step we take, whether we're consciously aware of it or not.

•God is with you when you go to school.

•God is with you when you're on the playground.

•God is with you when you go to bed at night.

•God is with you even if there are no other people around.

God is so close to us, it's as if He is holding our hands every minute of the day (Isaiah 41:13).

Sharing Time: God's Strong Hands

Sandra Crosser tells a wonderful story that illustrates how God is always with us.

When I was a little girl, I thought my dad was the strongest person in the world. He had strong arms and strong, big hands. When my dad took me places that were crowded and busy with lots of people and lots of cars, I would be a little bit afraid. Then my dad would hold my little hand in his big, strong hand. When Dad held my hand, I knew I would be safe.

Now I'm grown up. But sometimes my dad will still take my hand in his big, strong hand. When my dad holds my hand,

I know he loves me. Holding hands makes us feel safe and loved. But sometimes when I am all alone and afraid and need to feel safe and loved, my dad isn't there to hold my hand. (Hold up the Bible.)

In the Bible, almost in the middle, God wrote a special message to you and me. It's a message about holding hands. Listen as I read Isaiah 41:13: "For I am the LORD, your God, who takes hold of your right hand and says to you, Do not fear; I will help you."

Did you know that God holds your hand in His big, strong hand? You can always feel safe. You can always feel loved because God holds your hand.[2]

God Is All-Knowing

God knows everything.

"Great is our Lord and mighty in power; his understanding has no limit" (Psalm 147:5).

God is all-knowing. He knows all things: past (Isaiah 41:22), present (Hebrews 4:13), and future (Isaiah 46:10). And because He knows all things, there can be no increase or decrease in His knowledge.

One of the wonderful things about God being all-knowing is that He can never discover anything in our lives that will cause Him to change His mind about us being in His family. When we became Christians, God was fully aware of every sin we had ever committed and would ever commit in the future. That God knows everything about us and *accepts us anyway* should give every child of God a profound sense of security.

Sharing Time: Every Everything

If we could find the smartest doctor in the whole world, he would know a lot about the human body. Probably more than any other person. But would he know *every* everything there is to know about the human body? No, only God knows everything about it.

If we could talk to the zookeeper of the world's largest zoo, he would know a lot about all kinds of animals. Probably more than any other person. But would he know *every* everything there is to know about animals? No, only God knows every everything about them.

If we could visit the gardener of the most beautiful garden in the world, he would know a lot about plants. Probably more than any other person. But would he know *every* everything there is to know about plants? No, only God knows every everything about them.

Do you see where I'm going with this story? Even if you're the smartest, most knowledgeable person in the world, you can't know everything. Only God knows everything.

Isn't it great that we are part of the family of the One who knows it all!

God Loves You

God loves you always and forever!

"*God is love*" (1 John 4:8).

God isn't just characterized by love. He is the very *personification* of love (1 John 4:8). Love virtually permeates His being. And His love is not dependent upon the loveliness of the object (human beings). God loves us despite the fact that we are fallen in sin (John 3:16). (God loves the sinner, though He hates the sin.) And God loves all people equally, regardless of what they look like or where they live.

Sharing Time: Who Does God Love?

Some of your stuffed animals are very new and fluffy; others are very old and worn. Do you still love those old, raggedy stuffed animals? Of course you do. In fact, the reason they're so ragged is because you've slept with them and played with them so many times. Of course, you love your new stuffed animals, too. But just because some of your animals are looking worn and tattered doesn't mean you don't still love them.

In the same way, some people look "new and fluffy" and others may be more "old and shabby." Some people have a tooth missing; some people have lost their hair. Some people can't walk and must use wheelchairs. Some people have nice clothes while others have not-so-nice clothes. There are all kinds of people in the world.

But you know what? God loves *all* people just the same. God loves people with hair or without hair, with nice clothes or not-so-nice clothes, with teeth or missing teeth.

We need to be like God and love all people![3]

Loving God

 The first and greatest commandment is to love God with all of our being.

> *"'Love the Lord your God with all your heart and with all your soul and with all your mind.' This is the first and greatest commandment"* (Matthew 22:37,38).

The supreme business of life is to come to love the one true God with all our heart, mind, and strength. I believe it is in the home where this love for God is to be instilled in the child. The home is a school of spirituality where the child's love for God is born and nurtured through the years. It is not enough for parents to simply teach this to their children. They must also *live* it before their children. They must display a warmth and richness in their relationship with God before they can hope to impart it to their children.

Sharing Time: A Heart for God

For this illustration, cut out the shape of a heart—preferably on red paper—and then cut the heart into four equal-size pieces. Put the four pieces together on the floor.

Did you know that God wants us to love Him with all of our heart? It's true. He doesn't want us to use just *part* of our heart to love Him. He wants us to use *all* of it.

If we love God a lot but not completely, we're not loving God with all of our heart. (*Remove one piece of the heart.*)

If we love God some but not a lot, we're not loving God with all of our heart. (*Remove another piece.*)

If we love God just a little, we're not loving God with all of our heart. (*Remove another piece.*)

God wants us to love Him with *all* of our heart. (*Put the pieces back.*)

Will you love God with all of your heart?[4]

Depending on God

None of us can make it in life without God's help.

> *"Trust in the Lord with all your heart and lean not on your own understanding; in all your ways acknowledge him, and he will make your paths straight"* (Proverbs 3:5,6).

Help your children understand that they are going to require help, wisdom, and guidance far beyond themselves and their own abilities all their lives. No one is competent in themselves to live life. Life is just too big for any of us to handle alone.

In the early years of children's lives, they depend entirely upon mom and dad. Parents are the need-providers. But during these years, parents need to model for their children the fact that *they, too, are dependent—upon God*. Parents can and must teach their children to depend on the ultimate provider—God.

Sharing Time: God Takes Care of Us

Right now Mom and Dad take care of you, don't we! We give you food to eat, clothes to wear, and a place to live in. We take care of all your needs. And we love taking care of you in that way.

But you know what? You won't stay a child forever. You will grow up. And eventually, after you grow up, you'll be able to move out on your own and have your own house or apartment.

Now, it's important for you to realize that because you are a Christian you are a child of God. And as God's child, He always wants you to depend on Him. He's your heavenly Father. So, even when you're all grown-up, you'll depend on God for things like food to eat, clothes to wear, and a house to live in.

That's what mom and dad do. We depend on God to give us all these things. Let's not forget! When we turn to our heavenly father, He always takes care of us![5]

4

The True Jesus

"Christianity is not devotion to work, or
to a cause, or a doctrine, but devotion to
a person, the Lord Jesus Christ."[1]
—*Oswald Chambers*

Jesus asked one of His disciples, "Who do you say I am?"
This is one of the most important questions in all history.
Who is Jesus Christ? Christianity stands or falls on the identity and work of Jesus Christ. Whatever else we do as parents, we must make sure our children understand precisely
who Jesus is.

Jesus Is God

Jesus is and always has been God.

*"We wait for the blessed hope—the glorious ap-
pearing of our great God and Savior, Jesus Christ"*
(Titus 2:13).

Today, many people challenge the idea that Jesus is God.
As your kids grow up, they will often be confronted with the
claim that Jesus was not God but was just a good man, a
moral man, or a great teacher. The Scriptures, however, say
that *Jesus is God*.

Before becoming a man, Jesus had forever been God
(John 8:58). But when He was born from the womb of the

Virgin Mary (Luke 2:5-7), He was both God *and* man. He didn't give up His divine nature when He became a man. It is therefore right to say that Jesus, following His human birth, was *100-percent God* and *100-percent man*.

From a biblical perspective, to *know* Jesus is to know God. To *see* Jesus is to see God. To *believe* in Jesus is to believe in God. To *receive* Jesus is to receive God. To *honor* Jesus is to honor God. To *worship* Jesus is to worship God.

Among the things you will want to emphasize to your children are:

- Jesus is referred to in the Bible as God (Hebrews 1:8).

- Jesus has all the attributes (or characteristics) of God. For example, He's all-powerful (Matthew 28:18) and all-knowing (John 1:48).

- Jesus does things that only God can do, such as creating the entire universe (John 1:3) and raising people from the dead (John 11:43,44).

- Jesus was worshiped as God by those who came to know Him (Matthew 14:33).

Jesus Is Real

Jesus isn't pretend. He is real.

"We did not follow cleverly invented stories when we told you about the power and coming of our Lord Jesus Christ, but we were eyewitnesses of his majesty" (2 Peter 1:16).

Help your kids understand that Jesus is not like a cartoon figure that is make-believe. Jesus is God, and He became a real human being. He existed in history. He was actually born as a baby in a manger, grew up, and performed many incredible miracles during His three-year ministry. He also physically resurrected from the dead. These are not fairy-tale stories.

Sharing Time: The True Superhero!

I know that you've heard of lots of cartoon superheroes. You've heard of Superman, right? Well, on TV it looks like Superman has special powers. But Superman is just pretend. He's a make-believe person. He's not real.

You've heard of Batman, right? On TV it looks like Batman has special powers. But Batman is just pretend. He's a make-believe person. He's not real.

You've heard of Spiderman, right? On TV it looks like Spiderman has special powers. But Spiderman is just pretend. He's a make-believe person. He's not real.

Jesus is not pretend or make-believe. He is real. And when the Bible talks about Jesus doing incredible miracles, you can believe that those things really happened because *Jesus is God.*

Jesus Is Messiah-God

Jesus' miracles proved that He is God.

"Jesus did many other miraculous signs in the presence of his disciples, which are not recorded in this book. But these are written that you may believe that Jesus is the Christ, the Son of God, and that by believing you may have life in his name" (John 20:30,31).

John's Gospel always refers to the miracles of Jesus as "signs" (see John 4:54; 6:14; 9:16). Signs *always* signify something. Jesus' signs were strategically performed to signify His true identity and glory as God. Here are just a few of Jesus' signs or miracles and ways to talk about them with your children:

- Jesus turned water into wine (John 2:1-11). (Ask your children: *Do you know anyone but God who can turn water into wine?*)

- Jesus multiplied five small loaves of bread and two small fish into enough food to satisfy more than 5,000 people (John 6:5-14). (*Do you know anyone but God who can make a lot of food from a little bit of food?*)

- Jesus healed an invalid (John 5:3-9), a blind man (9:1-7), and many others. (*Do you know anyone but God who can heal people instantly?*)

- Jesus raised Lazarus from the dead (John 11:1-44). (*Do you know anyone but God that can raise people from the dead?*)

In each miracle Jesus performed, He distinguished Himself from weak and mortal man and attested to His true identity as Messiah-God. (The word "messiah" comes from an Old Testament Hebrew word meaning "anointed one." It is a counterpart to the New Testament word for Christ. Jesus is the Christ and the Messiah.)

Sharing Time: What Signs Tell Us

Do you know what a hospital is? It's where sick people can go to get taken care of by doctors and nurses.

If we were trying to figure out which building in our city is the hospital building, there are many signs that could tell us so. For one thing, there's a sign on the front of the building that says "Hospital." Also, many things happen there day and night that are signs to us that the building is indeed the hospital. For example:

- Doctors and nurses go in and out of the building each day.

- Ambulances drive to this building throughout the day and night.

- Sick people go into this building every day.

- Pregnant ladies go into the hospital with a baby in their "tummy" and leave the hospital with a baby in their arms.

Seeing all these things with our own eyes lets us know for sure that this building really is a hospital.

In the same way, we can know for sure that Jesus really is God. Besides Jesus' claim that He was God, people in Bible times saw signs with their own eyes that *proved* that Jesus is God. They saw Jesus do miracles that only God can do. So there's no doubt about it—Jesus really is God!

Jesus Fulfilled Prophecy

Jesus fulfilled all the Old Testament predictions about the coming birth of the Savior!

> *"Everything must be fulfilled that is written about me in the Law of Moses, the Prophets and the Psalms"* (Luke 24:44).

There are virtually hundreds of prophecies in the Old Testament that point to Jesus Christ. The fact that Jesus literally fulfilled all these prophecies indicates that He is who He claimed to be—the promised Messiah.

Sharing Time: Predicting the Future

We know *some* things that will happen before they happen, don't we?

- We know that at nighttime it will get dark because that's what happens every day.

- We know the sun will rise tomorrow morning because that's what happens every day.

- We know we will eventually get hungry again, even though we had a good breakfast, because that's what happens every day.

It's easy for us to know that these things will happen since they happen every day.

But in the Old Testament, God told us about things that would happen that had never happened before. That's not easy to do. In fact, only God can do that.

In the Old Testament, God tells us what's going to happen before it happens by using prophecies. Hundreds of these prophecies speak about Jesus. For example:

- God told us that Jesus would be born in Bethlehem (Micah 5:2).

- God told us that Jesus would do many miracles (Isaiah 35:5,6).

- God told us that Jesus would die on the cross for our sins (Psalm 22:1; Isaiah 53).

- God told us that Jesus would rise from the dead (Psalm 16:10).

And He told us these facts *before* Jesus was born on earth! These, and virtually hundreds of other prophecies, were fulfilled in Jesus Christ. That means Jesus is a special person, doesn't it? No one else fulfilled all those Old Testament prophecies like Jesus did. Jesus really is the Messiah that God told us about in the Old Testament.

Jesus Is Our Savior

Jesus came to die on the cross for our sins. He is our Savior.

"Today in the town of David a Savior has been born to you; he is Christ the Lord" (Luke 2:11).

The Bible tells us that after God created Adam and Eve, they sinned against God (we'll talk more about this in the next chapter). This posed a problem for God.

How could God remain holy and just and punish man's sin and, at the same time, forgive man and allow man back into His presence?

The answer is found in Jesus. Jesus came as our beloved Savior and died on the cross *on our behalf* (Matthew 20:28). He took our punishment. Those who believe in Him are forgiven of all their sins (Acts 16:31).

Christ was our substitute. He took our place. He took our sin upon Himself and provided salvation for us.

Sharing Time: The Great Exchange

There is a story about a small boy who was consistently late in coming home from school. One day his parents warned him that he must be home on time that afternoon. Nevertheless he arrived later than ever.

His mother met him at the door and said nothing. His father met him in the living room and said nothing.

At dinner that night, the boy looked at his plate. There was a small slice of bread and a cup of water. He looked at his father's full plate of food and then at his father, but his father remained silent. The boy was very sad.

The father waited for a moment. Then, out of his great love for the boy, he took the boy's plate and placed it in front of himself. He took his own plate—full of meat and potatoes—and put it in front of the boy. Then he smiled at his son.

When that boy grew up and became a man, he said, "All my life I've known what God is like by what my father did that night."[2]

This is kind of like what Christ did for us: He took what was *ours* (sin) and gave us what was *His* (salvation).

Christ Is Our Redeemer

Explain to your child that in Old Testament times, the phrase "kinsman-redeemer" was always used by a person who was related by blood to someone he was seeking to redeem from bondage or jail. If someone was sold into slavery, for example, it was the duty of a blood relative—the "next of kin" (a brother or a cousin)—to act as that person's kinsman-redeemer and buy him out of slavery (Leviticus 25:47, 48).

Jesus is the kinsman-redeemer for sin-enslaved humanity. For Jesus to become a kinsman-redeemer, however, He had to become related *by blood* to the human race. This indicates the necessity of Jesus becoming a man. *Jesus became a man—* He took on human "flesh" (without giving up His deity)— *in order to redeem man* (Hebrews 2:14-16). And because Jesus was also fully God, His sacrificial death had infinite value (Hebrews 9:11-28).

The word "redemption" refers to "freedom by the payment of a price." The purchase price for our redemption from sin was the blood of Jesus. Because of what Christ accomplished at the cross, the believer is no longer a slave to sin and Satan.

Jesus' Resurrection

Death did not defeat Jesus. On the third day, He rose from the dead.

> *What I received I passed on to you as of first importance: that Christ died for our sins according to the Scriptures, that he was buried, that he was raised on the third day according to the Scriptures"* (1 Corinthians 15:3,4).

It is true that Jesus died on a cross. This may cause your young one to wonder how it can be that Jesus is alive today if He died on a cross. This is where the doctrine of the resurrection comes in. Jesus died, but three days later He came to life again. Here is one way to share the truth about the resurrection:

> When Jesus died, His followers were very sad. But imagine how overjoyed they were when they saw that He had risen from the dead. And because Jesus has risen from

the dead, all those who believe in Him will one day be raised from the dead. Jesus overcame death.

Do you know how we know for sure that Jesus resurrected from the dead? The Bible tells us He did:

- The tomb Jesus was buried in was empty (Luke 24:1-3).

- The risen Jesus showed His disciples "his hands and side" (John 20:20).

- The resurrected Jesus ate three different times with His disciples (Luke 24:28-30, 41-43; John 21:10-13).

- Jesus bodily appeared to more than 500 people at the same time following His resurrection (1 Corinthians 15:6).

- Jesus made numerous other appearances to people (for example, see Matthew 28:1-10 and Luke 24:1-11).

Sharing Time: New Life

At Easter time we have lots of brightly colored Easter eggs, don't we? Did you know that these eggs remind us of Jesus' resurrection? They do.

What hatches from an egg? A bird does. One moment the egg is just sitting there. Then it starts to shake as the baby bird moves inside it. Next he pokes a hole in the shell of the egg and comes out. *The egg represents new life.*

This reminds us of what happened to Jesus. He was crucified for our sins, and He died on the cross. He was then buried in a tomb. But three days later new life came into His body and He was resurrected from the dead. Jesus defeated death. He was more powerful than death.[3]

The empty shell of the egg reminds us of the empty tomb!

Jesus Is Not One of Many Ways to God

Jesus is the *only* way to a relationship with God.

"Jesus answered, 'I am the way and the truth and

> the life. No one comes to the Father except through
> me' " (John 14:6).

> *"Salvation is found in no one else, for there is no
> other name under heaven given to men by which we
> must be saved"* (Acts 4:12).

Some people claim that Jesus is just "one of many ways
to God." This line of thinking argues that all the leaders of
all the world religions point to the same God. This is not true,
however. The reason we can say this is that the leaders of the
different religions had different (and contradictory) ideas
about God. For example,

- Jesus taught that there is only one God (Matthew 28:19).

- Confucius believed in many gods.

- Zoroaster taught that there is both a good god and a bad
  god.

- Buddha taught that the concept of God was irrelevant.

Obviously, these religious leaders are not pointing to the
same God we know. If one is right, all the others are wrong.
If Jesus was right *(and He is)*, then all the others are wrong.

Jesus claimed that what He said took precedence over all
others. He said He is humanity's *only* means of coming into
a relationship with God (see John 14:6). And this was con-
firmed by those who followed Him (Acts 4:12; 1 Timothy 2:5).

It's important to understand that Jesus is totally unique.
He proved that all He said was true by resurrecting from the
dead (see Acts 17:31). None of the other leaders of the different world religions did that. Jesus' resurrection proved
that He was who He claimed to be—the divine Messiah (Romans 1:4).

You might ask your child, How many right answers are
there to the question, "What is 1 plus 1?" Two is the only possible answer. In the same way, there's only one possible answer to the question, Who is the Savior? It's Jesus Christ.

Sharing Time: Jesus Came to Save Us

If you received a Christmas card from God, what do you think it would say?

Would it just say, "Have a merry Christmas"? I don't think so.

Would it just say, "Have a happy new year"? I don't think so.

Would it just say, "Happy holidays"? I don't think so.

Instead, I think the card might have a very important verse from the Bible: "Here is a trustworthy saying that deserves full acceptance: Christ Jesus came into the world to save sinners" (1 Timothy 1:15).

Jesus is the *only* one who can save us. That's why He came into the world.[4] There are not a lot of saviors in the world. *There is only Jesus.*

Aren't you thankful that Jesus came into the world to save us?

5

All About Sin and Salvation

"I remember two things: that I am a great
sinner and that Christ is a great Savior."[1]
— *John Newton*

Suppose you have an ailment and you go to the doctor.
The only way to get the right treatment is to first have an accurate diagnosis. An incorrect diagnosis leads to the wrong
cure. Similarly, the only way to have an accurate cure for the
spiritual ills of humankind is to first have an accurate diagnosis of man's spiritual state. God diagnosed man as having
a serious sin problem. The cure for this "disease" is believing
in the Savior Jesus Christ, who died for our sins at the cross.

Let's start at the beginning and find out where man's
spiritual problems began.

Adam and Eve's Sin

We are all born with a sin nature.

*"Through the disobedience of the one man the many
were made sinners"* (Romans 5:19).

After God created Adam and Eve, He immediately initi-
ated a personal relationship with them (you can read about
this in Genesis, chapters 1–3). Unfortunately, Adam and Eve
severed that relationship in the fall. They sinned against God.

163

Help your children understand that when Adam and Eve sinned, they broke their relationship and fellowship with God, and sin and rebellion against God was introduced into them and through them into all their descendants (Romans 5:12). This sin nature is the source of all our individual acts of sin and is the major reason why we are rendered unfit for a relationship with a holy God (Ephesians 2:1-3).

Adam's initial sin, then, caused him to fall, and he became an entirely different being from a moral standpoint. Every child of Adam is born with the Adamic nature and is always prone to sin. It remains an active force in every Christian's life (Romans 8:4; Galatians 5:16,17).

Sharing Time: Jesus, the Stain Remover!

What might happen if you put on a nice pair of white pants and a white shirt and went outside to play in the dirt and grass? Do you think you might get some grass stains on your clothes? I think so. Do you think you might get some dirt stains on your clothes? I think so.

Some of those stains might be so bad that even washing them in a washing machine won't get them out. Some of those stains might be stuck on your clothes forever.

Did you know that the Bible teaches that each one of us is born into the world with a stain on us? It's the stain of sin. Each one of us is born with a stain of sin that God does not like to see. This stain of sin came into the world when the first man and woman, Adam and Eve, sinned against God. Ever since then, all of us have had a stain of sin on us.[2]

I'm very thankful for Jesus because He came into the world to die for our sins. When we believe in Him, He forgives our sins. And He makes us *white as snow*. Jesus is our stain remover!

The Penalty for Sin

Sin separates us from God.

"Your iniquities have separated you from your God; your sins have hidden his face from you, so that he will not hear" (Isaiah 59:2).

When Adam and Eve sinned, they passed immediately into a state of being spiritually separated from God. They were kicked out of the Garden of Eden and a sword-bearing angel was posted to guard it. Their expulsion from the Garden gave geographical expression to humankind's spiritual separation from God (Genesis 3:23).

Emphasize to your children that people *still* sin, *still* defy authority, and *still* act independently of God. A great gulf exists between sinful man and God (Isaiah 59:2). Twentieth-century men and women, boys and girls are no different from Adam and Eve. We may have added some sophisticated technology, built a few tall skyscrapers, and written millions of books, but there is still a chasm between sinful man and a holy God.

Our stain of sin blots out God's face from us as effectively as the clouds do the sun. Until our sins are forgiven, we are exiles far from our true home. We have no communion with God. But Jesus Christ is the "bridge" that restores that communion.

Sharing Time: Our Bridge to God

Imagine a rapidly flowing river separating two pieces of land. The river is too deep for us to walk to the other side. And the water is flowing much too fast for us to swim across or take a boat across. The only way to cross the river would be if there were a bridge going across the river to the other side.

Because of our sin against God, it's like there is a giant river between us and God. There's no way to get to the other side. We are separated. We need a bridge. The good news is that even though we can't get to the other side by ourselves, Jesus is our "bridge." By His death on the cross, He has provided a crossing for us to use to have a restored relationship with God.

Sin: Missing the Target

None of us can measure up to God's perfect standard. We are all sinners.

"All have sinned and fall short of the glory of God" (Romans 3:23).

A key meaning of sin is "missing the target." *All* of us miss the target. There is not a single person in the world who is capable of fulfilling all of God's laws at all times. All of us are sinners because of our failure to obey God's law.

Sharing Time: Jumping to the Moon

Pretend you've got two of your friends over to play and you're all going to try to jump to the moon. One of you may be able to jump a little higher than the other two. But can you even come close to jumping to the moon? *No way!*

No matter how high you jump—even if you were an Olympic gold medalist in the high jump—you fall hopelessly short of the moon.

It's the same way with our lives. We all miss the target. We all break God's laws. We all fall short of God's perfect standards. And because of that we need a Savior.

The Problem God Faced

When man sinned, here are the problems God faced:

- How could a holy and just God forgive the sinner and allow the sinner into His presence?

- Whereas God's justice burned in wrath against man for outraging His holiness, God's love equally yearned to find a way to forgive him and bring him back into fellowship with Himself.

- But how could God express His love, His righteousness, and His justice toward man *all at the same time*? He could send His son.

The good news of the Gospel is that Jesus died on the cross for our sins. He took our place. He took our punishment. And because of what Jesus did at the cross, you and I can now receive the free gift of salvation.

Salvation Is a Free Gift

 Salvation is a gift from God. It is not something that can be earned.

"For it is by grace you have been saved, through faith—and this not from yourselves, it is the gift of God—not by works, so that no one can boast" (Ephesians 2:8,9).

God's gift of salvation is a grace-gift. The word "grace" means undeserved favor. Because salvation is a grace-gift, it can't be earned. *It's free!* We can't attain it by a good performance. Titus 3:5 tells us that God "saved us, not on the basis of deeds which we have done in righteousness, but according to His mercy"(NASB). Our efforts to save ourselves are futile. It cannot be done. No matter how hard we try, it is of no use because God's standard is perfection. The source of salvation lies in God's grace, not in exertions of will-power, or in efforts of discipline, or any other self-effort. *Salvation is a free gift!*

Help your children understand that a gift must be accepted for what it is: something freely given and unmerited.

If you have to pay for a gift or do something to deserve or earn it, it is not really a gift. True gifts are freely given and freely received. To attempt to give or receive a gift in any other manner makes it not a gift.

It is the same way with our salvation in Jesus Christ. God offers us salvation as a free gift based on what Jesus did for us at the cross. God does not attach strings to salvation because to do so would make it something other than a gift. Any attempt on our part (no matter how small) to pay for our salvation by *doing* something is an insult to God.

Sharing Time: The Best Gift of All

In order to make the following point, you will need to obtain a picture (painting) of Jesus and wrap it up like a Christmas gift.

It's fun to give gifts to one another, isn't it? We give gifts to each other at Christmastime and at birthdays. It's a nice way of saying "I love you."

Did you know that God has given us a very special gift? He gave us this gift because He loves us so much.

(Open the package and pull out the picture of Jesus.)

The most precious gift God has given us is His Son, Jesus Christ. Jesus came to earth to die on the cross in order to give us the gift of salvation.

Salvation is a free gift. We can't pay God for it. It's too expensive. I think you'll agree with me that this is the best possible gift anyone could ever receive.[3]

Receiving the Gift Through Faith

The way we receive the free gift of salvation from God is by faith in Jesus Christ.

"Believe in the Lord Jesus, and you will be saved" (Acts 16:31).

God has not made the gospel complicated. It is quite easy to enter into a relationship with Jesus. In fact, according to the New Testament, one enters into this relationship by placing simple faith in Jesus.

This may sound too good to be true, yet it is the clear teaching of Scripture. Some people try to add specific good "works" as a condition for salvation, but this goes against Scripture. The Bible portrays salvation as a free gift we receive by faith alone.

Placing faith in Jesus Christ simply involves taking Christ at His word. Faith involves believing that Christ was who He said He was. Faith also involves believing that Christ can do what He claimed He could do—He can forgive us and come into our lives. (You may want to review "Evangelizing Your Children" in "Teach Your Children Well" for more on all this.)

Salvation and Forgiveness

 Though we don't deserve it, God completely forgives us of all our sins the moment we place faith in Jesus Christ.

"Their sins and lawless acts I will remember no more" (Hebrews 10:17).

"You will again have compassion on us; you will tread our sins underfoot and hurl all our iniquities into the depths of the sea" (Micah 7:19).

"For as high as the heavens are above the earth, so great is his love for those who fear him; as far as the east is from the west, so far has he removed our transgressions from us" (Psalm 103:11,12).

Look at that last verse again. There is a definite point that is "north" and another that is "south" (the North and South Poles). But there are no such points for "east" and "west." It doesn't matter how far you go to the east; you will never arrive where east begins because by definition, east is the opposite of west. The two never meet. They never will meet and never could meet because they are defined as opposites.

To remove our sins "as far as the east is from the west" is, by definition, to put them where no one can ever find them. That is the forgiveness God has granted us! Though it may be hard for our children (and even us) to understand, God is able to forget our past. God throws our sins into the depths of the sea and puts up a sign on the shore that reads "No fishing!"

Psalm 130:3,4 says, "If you, O LORD, kept a record of sins, O Lord, who could stand? But with you there is forgiveness." The phrase "kept a record" was an accounting term in Old Testament times. It referred to keeping an itemized account. The psalmist's point is that if we think God is keeping a detailed account of our sins, there would be no way for us to have a relationship with Him. It would be impossible. The good news is that God does not keep an itemized account but forgives those who trust in Christ.

Sharing Time: God's Eraser

I need your help with a mistake I've made. I've been writing a letter to a friend on this piece of paper, and I spelled a word wrong. My friend gave me this (*hold up an eraser*), but she didn't tell me what I should do with it. Can you help me?

(*Your child will tell you it's for erasing mistakes on paper.*)

Oh, that's great. Now that I've erased my mistake, I can write the word correctly. Thanks for helping me. Now my letter is perfect.

Did you know that God has a kind of eraser, too? You see, because Jesus died for our sins at the cross, God forgives us for all our sins when we believe in Jesus. It's almost as if God took a big eraser and erased all the sins out of our lives. Isn't that great?[4]

Because of what Jesus did for us, we are just like a perfect letter to God, a letter with no mistakes on it. Our lives are clean from mistakes and sins.

Sharing Time: "Cleared" by God

You need to have a calculator for this illustration.

See this little calculator? Look what I can do if I make a mistake. I can press the clear button, and automatically the numbers I entered go away. Then I can begin again with no mistakes. The calculator completely forgets my mistake.

That's what happens to our sins when God forgives us. One of the blessings of salvation is that our sins are totally forgiven. It's like God says in Hebrews 10:17: "Their sins and lawless acts I will remember no more."

Security of Salvation

God never kicks us out of His forever family. We are secure in our salvation.

> *"I give them eternal life, and they shall never perish; no one can snatch them out of my hand. My Father, who has given them to me, is greater than all; no one can snatch them out of my Father's hand"* (John 10:28-30).

We are secure in our salvation! We know this for several reasons.

For one thing, we are told that the Father keeps us in His sovereign hands, and no one can take us out of them (John 10:28-30). God has us in His firm grip. And that grip will never let us go.

And the Lord Jesus regularly prays for us (Hebrews 7:25). As our divine High Priest, His work of intercessory prayer is necessary because of our weaknesses, our helplessness, and our immaturity as children of God. He knows our limitations, and He knows the power and the strategy of the foe with whom we have to contend (Satan). Therefore, He is faithful in making intercession for us.

There are many other verses that talk about our security in salvation. We will look at some of these later in the book.

God's Provision: Power and Protection

1

The Family of God—The Church

"A church is a hospital for sinners, not a museum for saints."[1]

—*L.L. Nash*

I have vivid childhood memories of going to church on Sundays with my family. There were 10 of us. We would often draw stares from people as we filled up an entire pew!

Among the many things I appreciate about my parents is that they were always committed to making sure we went to church. We knew plenty of families who stayed home Sundays. But the days we missed going to church were few and far between.

What Is the Church?

The church is "the ever-enlarging body of born-again believers who comprise the universal Body of Christ over whom He reigns as Lord."[2] Although the members of the church may differ in age, sex, race, wealth, social status, and ability, they are all joined together as *one people* (Galatians 3:28). All of them share in one Spirit and worship one Lord (Ephesians 4:3-6). This body is comprised of only believers in Christ. The way you become a member of this universal body is to simply place faith in Jesus Christ. If you're a believer, you're in!

The church involves two very important relationships: relationships with other Christians, and a corporate relationship with the Lord Jesus. One relationship affects the other. Consider:

- Not attending church and worshiping with other Christians can have a negative impact on our relationship with the Lord. (He *wants* us to attend church and worship Him.)

- If we don't have a good relationship with the Lord it can affect the way we treat other Christians.

So, it's important that we teach our children to take *both* relationships very seriously.

Fellowshiping with Believers

 Gathering together with other Christians is a source of strength for us.

"Therefore encourage one another and build each other up, just as in fact you are doing" (1 Thessalonians 5:11).

God does not want us to be "Lone Ranger" Christians. He designed the church for our benefit. Christian fellowship and sharing should be the family activity of God's people in the local church. This gathering together for fellowshiping and sharing gives strength to the people of God. John Wesley, the founder of Methodism, said, "There is nothing more unchristian than a solitary Christian."[3] C.S. Lewis similarly commented, "The New Testament does not envisage solitary religion. Some kind of regular assembly for worship and instruction is everywhere taken for granted in the Epistles. So we must be regular practicing members of the church."[4]

| Sharing Time: Keeping Hot and Glowing |

Cookouts are fun, aren't they? It's fun to put charcoals in the grill, light them on fire, and watch them as they slowly become glowing hot. When the coals are good and hot, it makes it much easier to cook our hamburgers quickly.

As long as all the coals stay close together, they stay hot and keep glowing. But what happens if you move one of the coals off to the side, away from the other coals? It cools down and stops glowing. The coals have to stay next to each other to stay hot.

That's kind of like it is at church. As long as we stay close to other Christians at church, we stay warm in our spiritual lives. But if we stop going to church, we cool off.

God wants us to go to church and stay close to other Christians. That will help us be the kind of people God wants us to be. It will help us stay warm in our devotion to Him.

Equipping the Saints in Church

Pass It On

The church equips members for the work of ministry.

"It was he who gave some to be apostles, some to be prophets, some to be evangelists, and some to be pastors and teachers, to prepare God's people for works of service, so that the body of Christ may be built up" (Ephesians 4:11,12).

A church is healthy and growing to the degree that individual church members are being equipped for the work of ministry. The church should not be a place where the pastor or minister does all the work. Every member of the church should be involved in some kind of ministry, and the church is where they become trained and equipped to carry out their service. We might say the church is a spiritual training center for Christians.

Sharing Time: "Body" Building

Do you know what a gym is? It's a place where people go to exercise. The more that people exercise in the gym, the bigger all their muscles get and the more their bodies are built up. This is called body building.

Have you ever seen someone with really big muscles? That person probably goes to the gym a lot.

In a way, the church is God's body-building program. As we go to church, our spiritual muscles get bigger and bigger. Our mind power grows strong as we are filled with God's Word. Our heart for Christ expands with love for God. At church we become equipped to serve God.

Salt and Light

Believers are to be salt and light in the world.

"You are the salt of the earth . . . You are the light of the world" (Matthew 5:13,14).

The church is a place where members become ready to make an impact on the world. Every believer can be used by God to influence the world. Jesus said, "You are the salt of the earth." Salt is known for its effectiveness as a preservative. We are to have a preserving effect on the world by influencing it for Christ.

Jesus also said, "You are the light of the world. A city on a hill cannot be hidden." Jesus did not call us to be "secret agent" Christians. We are not to cloak our lights. Because the darkness of our world is hovering over humanity as never before, there has never been a time when the light of each individual Christian has been more needed. As evangelist Billy Graham put it, "The Christian should stand out like a sparkling diamond."[5]

Sharing Time: Growing Strong to Share Jesus

Do you know what a greenhouse is? A greenhouse is a very special building where you grow plants. Inside this house, it's just the right temperature for plants to grow. There's just enough water given to each of the plants. There's just enough sunlight that comes in through special windows. Everything is just right so the plants can grow. Once the plants are grown, they can be used to make the world more beautiful.

The church is kind of like a greenhouse for people. Inside the church we grow spiritually, and everything in the church is just right for our spiritual growth. There's Bible-reading, singing songs, worshiping God, Sunday school, and much more. By going to church, we grow strong as Christians.

When we grow strong as Christians, we can be a good influence on the world around us—just like plants make the world more beautiful. Once we grow strong we can be like "salt" and "light" in the world. That makes God happy.[6]

Every Member Involved!

Every member is a "minister" who can use his or her gifts to serve others.

"The eye cannot say to the hand, 'I don't need you!' And the head cannot say to the feet, 'I don't need you!' " (1 Corinthians 12:21).

One reason it's so important for each person to be involved in church is that we need each other. Every member of the church has unique gifts and talents given to him or her by God, and he or she can render service in ways that no one else can. That's the way God designed it. Each part of the body of Christ is important (1 Corinthians 12:1-20). Let me illustrate.

Mountain climbers, for safety reasons, rope themselves together when climbing a mountain. That way, if one climber slips and falls, he won't fall to his death. He'll be held by the others until he can regain his footing.

This is the way God designed the church to be. When one believer slips and falls, the others can hold him up until he regains his footing. Believers in the church are to make every effort to minister to individual members (Hebrews 10:24) and care for the needy in their midst (2 Corinthians 8–9).

Sharing Time: Part of the Team

You've played football before, right? It's a fun game to play. But let me ask you, How much fun would it be if you tried to play a football game all by yourself? That would be hard, wouldn't it. And it wouldn't be as much fun. It's much better if you have a football *team*, with lots of people involved.

Teamwork is also involved in church ministry. Wouldn't it be bad if the only person who did anything in the church was the pastor? That's not the way God intended it. God wants everyone to get involved—to be like a team. Each person on the team is important.[7]

Are you excited to be on the team at church?

Church: Our Service Station

God wants us to attend church regularly.

"Let us not give up meeting together, as some are in the habit of doing, but let us encourage one another—and all the more as you see the Day approaching" (Hebrews 10:25).

Current polls indicate that a massive realignment of the way people think is presently taking place all across America. What was formerly considered necessary by many is now being placed in the category of optional. Among items in transition from the necessary to the optional are church attendance, worship, prayer, and Bible reading.

Dorothy Bass, a Chicago Theological Seminary professor, says the declining interest in church is due to a failure "to transmit the meaning and excitement of Christianity from one generation to another, one person to another."[8] Bass is entirely correct. Many Christians today are simply not excited about their faith, and unexcited parents are passing this lack of interest on to their children. Ecclesiastical boredom is plaguing the modern American church on a massive level. It is obvious, then, that we as parents must do two things.

1. We must instill in our children the biblical view that we are not to "give up meeting together" (Hebrews 10:25; Ephesians 2:19; 1 Thessalonians 5:10,11; and 1 Peter 3:8).

2. We must ourselves be committed to the church and communicate our commitment to (and *excitement* for) the church to our kids. Our kids will derive their attitude toward the church largely from us. We are models; they are imitators.

Sharing Time: Spiritual Gas

Why is it necessary to go to the gas station? We go to put gas into our car. As we drive around we use up our gas again. We have to keep coming back to the gas station to get more gas. One trip to the gas station won't do it.

Well, you and I don't need gasoline, but we *do* need to be spiritually fed every week so we can keep going. We need to keep getting our hearts and heads filled with Jesus. And the place we go to get spiritually filled with Jesus is church.

If we stop taking our cars to the gas station, they eventually run out of gas and stop running. If we stop going to church, we run out of spiritual strength. For cars to run right, they have to have gas. For people to run right, they have to go to church and get filled with Jesus.[9]

2

Power from on High—
The Holy Spirit

"The Spirit's control will replace sin's
control. His power is greater than the
power of all your sin."[1]

—Erwin Lutzer

An American with an English gentleman was viewing
the Niagara whirlpool rapids, when he said to his friend:
"Come, and I'll show you the greatest unused power in the
world." Taking him to the foot of the Niagara falls, he said,
"*There* is the greatest unused power in the world!"

"Ah, no, my brother, not so!" was the reply. "The greatest
unused power in the world is the Holy Spirit of the living
God."[2]

The Holy Spirit is the power source for Christians.
Without the ministry of the Holy Spirit, it would be impossible for anyone to successfully live the Christian life. For this
reason, it is critically important that our children understand
what Scripture says about this important subject.

The Divine Comforter

The Holy Spirit lives in every believer. He is our
comforter.

*"I will ask the Father, and he will give you another
Counselor to be with you forever"* (John 14:16).

The word "counselor" in the above verse is a rich one, carrying the meaning of *comforter, helper, advocate, one who strengthens*. Thoughts of encouragement, support, assistance, care, and the shouldering of responsibility are all conveyed by this one word.

Notice that the Holy Spirit is called "*another* counselor." There are two New Testament Greek words that can be translated by the English word "another." The first one means "another of a *different* kind." The second means "another of the *same* kind." It is this second word that is used in John 14:16.

Jesus was saying that He would ask the Father to send another Helper *of the same kind as Himself*—a personal, ever-present helper. Just as Jesus was a personal comforter who helped the disciples for three years during His earthly ministry, so now Christ's followers would have another personal comforter—the Holy Spirit—who would be with them throughout their lives.

What a wonderful truth this is! We are never alone in our troubles. When life seems too much for us—when we encounter tough times or we're treated unfairly—we can rejoice in the presence of the Holy Spirit who comforts and encourages us.

Help your children grasp the significance of this. There is never a time when they're alone. The Holy Spirit is always with them.

Sharing Time: Our Forever Comforter

Hannah was a little girl who loved her teddy bear. She took the teddy bear with her everywhere she went. It sat next to her when she ate. It laid next to her when she took her naps and at nighttime. And when she went over to her friend's house to spend the night, she always brought it with her. Her teddy bear was her comforter.

One day Hannah went with her parents on a three-day trip. It was a fun trip—but Hannah forgot to bring her teddy bear with her. This made her sad. No teddy bear to sleep with. No teddy bear to eat with. How she missed her teddy bear.

Did you know that the Holy Spirit is also a Comforter? Did you know He stays with us day and night? You can't forget to bring Him either, because He is always with us— no matter where we go.

We can't see the Holy Spirit, but He's still there. And he doesn't wear out like our teddy bears do. He doesn't wear out because He is God.

Isn't it great that the Holy Spirit is always with us to bring us comfort?

The Holy Spirit's "Seal"

The Holy Spirit "seals" us—guaranteeing that we will make it all the way to heaven.

"Do not grieve the Holy Spirit of God, with whom you were sealed for the day of redemption" (Ephesians 4:30).

The apostle Paul informs us that at the moment of believing in Jesus, believers are marked "with a seal, the promised Holy Spirit" (Ephesians 1:13).

Sharing Time: Mailed to God

Way back in biblical times, when people sent letters to each other they would seal the envelope (or scroll) with wax.

At birthday parties, you've probably seen how wax melts after you light candles with a match, right? Well, ancient people used to melt wax right where you close the envelope, and when the wax dried it would keep the envelope shut.

When anybody saw a wax seal on an envelope, they knew that no one was supposed to open that letter except the person the letter was addressed to. So, if I were writing a letter to my friend Jane, that wax seal would mean that no one but Jane could open my letter.

The Bible says that you and I are "sealed" by the Holy Spirit. We are like a letter being delivered to God. The seal of the Holy Spirit guarantees that we will make it all the way to heaven. God promises us that!

Sharing Time: We Belong to God

In days past and often still today, cattle ranchers gather up all their young cows and put a mark called a "brand" on the cow's backside. Each rancher has his own special mark to put on the cows.

That mark on the young cow means that the cow belongs to that rancher. If somebody tries to steal that cow, the rancher can say, "See, this cow has my mark on it, so it's mine."

In the same way, God has put His special mark on each of us. It's the mark of the Holy Spirit. And this mark means that we belong to God. We are *His* property. And just like a rancher takes care of his cows, so God takes care of His property—*us!*

The Holy Spirit Controls Us

Scripture commands us to be filled with (controlled by) the Holy Spirit.

> *"Do not get drunk on wine, which leads to debauchery. Instead, be filled with the Spirit"* (Ephesians 5:18).

God says Christians are to be filled with the Spirit. In fact, they are to *keep on* being filled with the Spirit. We know this because the word "filled" in Ephesians 5:18 is a present tense verb. This indicates continuing action. Day by day, moment by moment, you and I are to be filled with the Spirit. But what does this mean?

The context provides us with the answer. Both drunk persons and spirit-filled persons are *controlled* persons. That is, they're under the influence of either liquor (in the former case) or the Spirit (in the latter case). This causes them to do things that are unnatural to them. In both cases, they abandon themselves to the influence of either the liquor or the Holy Spirit.

So, to be filled with the Holy Spirit means that one's life will be governed no longer by self but by the Holy Spirit. It is not a matter of acquiring more of the Spirit, but rather of the Spirit of God acquiring all of the individual. The filling of the Spirit is accomplished in the life of a believer when he or she is fully yielded to the indwelling Holy Spirit. This yieldedness results in a spiritual condition in which the Holy Spirit controls and empowers the individual moment by moment.

We need to progressively help our children understand this truth, for a proper relationship with the Holy Spirit is the key to a successful spiritual life. The Holy Spirit is the power source for spiritual living.

Sharing Time: Don't Crash!

When you're riding a bicycle, you control it with the handlebars, the pedals, and the brakes. You steer the bike very carefully so you stay on course. You use the pedals to make the bike go. You use the brakes to slow down when you go around curves so you won't crash. By doing these things you keep your bike under control.

What happens if you take your hands off the handlebars, and you take your feet off the pedals and brakes? The bike will get out of control, and you will soon crash.

Just as you control your bike when you're riding it, so the Holy Spirit can control your life when you let Him. As you yield to the Holy Spirit, He keeps your life on track. He keeps you on course. He helps take you around life's curves. He slows you down when you need to. As long as He's in control, your life won't crash.

It is wise to be filled with—or controlled by—the Holy Spirit.

Walking in the Spirit

 Live in dependence upon the Holy Spirit, and enjoy good spiritual fruits.

> *"So I say, live by the Spirit, and you will not gratify the desires of the sinful nature"* (Galatians 5:16).

> *"The fruit of the Spirit is love, joy, peace, patience, kindness, goodness, faithfulness, gentleness and self-control. Against such things there is no law"* (Galatians 5:22,23).

We can have victory over the sin nature that is inside us by walking—or living—in dependence upon the Holy Spirit. The word "live" in Galatians 5:16 is a present-tense verb. This indicates continuing action. We are to continually depend on the Spirit. As we do this, we will live in a way that is pleasing to God.

Constantly depending on the Spirit also produces spiritual fruit in our lives. The fruit of the Spirit includes love, joy, peace, patience, kindness, goodness, faithfulness, gentleness, and self-control. These qualities represent an accurate profile of Jesus. The character of our Lord is reproduced in our lives as we live under the control of the Spirit. We progressively take on the family likeness (as members of God's forever family) as we walk in the Spirit.

Sharing Time: Planted in the Holy Spirit

What happens if you put an apple seed in some soil with plenty of water and sunshine? It will grow into a beautiful apple tree. Eventually the tree will produce lots of nice apples. But the seed *depends* on the soil, water, and sunshine in order to grow right.

What would happen if we pulled the seed out of the ground and put it on the sidewalk? Would it grow? No, of course not! The seed needs soil, water, and sunshine in order to grow and bear good fruit.

Our lives are kind of like that seed. If our lives are "planted" in the soil of the Holy Spirit, and we live in dependence upon Him, our lives will produce lots of good fruit like love, joy, and peace. But if we don't depend on Him, our lives will not bear fruit. Instead we will be like that seed on the sidewalk.

Do you want to bear fruit in your life? As we depend on the Holy Spirit, our lives will bear plenty of fruit!

Spiritual Gifts

The Holy Spirit has given every believer one or more spiritual gifts to be used in serving the body of Christ.

> *"All these [gifts] are the work of one and the same Spirit, and he gives them to each one, just as he determines"* (1 Corinthians 12:11).

Kids love gifts! Help your child understand that the Holy Spirit bestows one or more spiritual gifts upon every single believer. What are some of these gifts? The apostle Paul explains,

> We have different gifts, according to the grace given us. If a man's gift is prophesying, let him use it in proportion to his faith. If it is serving, let him serve; if it is teaching, let him teach; if it is encouraging, let him encourage; if it is contributing to the needs of others, let him give generously; if it is leadership, let him govern diligently; if it is showing mercy, let him do it cheerfully (Romans 12:6-8; see also 1 Corinthians 12:8-10).

Sharing Time: Everyone Has a Job

God has given unique talents and gifts to each one of us. He wants us to use these gifts and talents to help and serve others.

The church is a lot like a human body. The arms are needed, just as the legs, back, stomach, head, eyes, mouth, nose, and so forth, are needed. All these parts work together in the human body. If any of the parts are missing, the body won't work as well as it could.

This is just like it is in the church. Just like the parts of the body are all important, so every member of the church is important. Each member has a gift from God to use in serving others.

Your children will inevitably wonder how they can discover what spiritual gift(s) they have. Tell them it's okay if they don't know right now. Let them know that as they grow up, they will discover their spiritual gift by serving in different areas in the body of Christ. As we involve ourselves in ministry, our spiritual gifts naturally surface.

3

Winning Battles— The World, the Sin Nature, and the Devil

"You must know your enemy before you can defeat him."

—Anonymous

Military strategists have long recognized that a large part of defeating an enemy is knowing the enemy. Only those who know the strategies of one's opponents stand a chance of defeating them.

There are three potent enemies aligned against those who seek to walk with Christ: the world, the sin nature, and the devil. Each one works in concert with the others to bring about the downfall of the Christian. It is critical for the Christian to recognize that this destructive trio does not fight fair. It is a gang attack. No matter where we go in the world, we are engaged in spiritual combat. There is no spiritual demilitarized zone. The whole planet is a battleground.

As parents, it is our duty to increasingly train our children (not necessarily in early childhood but certainly in their later childhood years) in how to deal with the world, the sin nature, and the devil. Their future well-being as Christians depends upon it.

Confronting the World

 We must be cautious about our interaction with the world, because it offers many distractions away from Christ.

"Do not love the world or anything in the world. If anyone loves the world, the love of the Father is not in him. For everything in the world—the cravings of sinful man, the lust of his eyes and the boasting of what he has and does—comes not from the Father but from the world" (1 John 2:15,16).

The word "world," when used in Scripture, often refers not to the physical planet Earth, but to an anti-God system headed by Satan. Indeed, 1 John 5:19 tells us that "the whole world is under the control of the evil one [Satan]." The world is portrayed in Scripture as a seducer. It perpetually seeks to distract our attention and devotion away from God. It seeks to eclipse our view of heavenly things. It can subtly trap us and lead us astray. For this reason, the New Testament instructs us not to love the world or anything in the world (see 1 John 2:15,16). But there are numerous things in the world that can appeal to our sin nature. If we give in to these things, our attention is drawn away from God. Embracing the world and its ways will inevitably drive our affections away from God. Before we were Christians, we followed the ways of the world without hesitation (Ephesians 2:2). But when we became Christians, we obtained another master—Jesus Christ —who calls us to be separate from the world. There is no neutral ground.

What are some of the things of the world that may entice us away from God? We may be enticed by money, material possessions, fame, a career, entertainment, and pleasure. The list goes on and on.

Emphasize to your child that no one thing in the above list is intrinsically wrong or evil. They do, however, have the *potential* to shift our attention away from Christ as our first priority. Any of these items can effectively sidetrack us into the web of worldliness. So be careful. Ask yourself these questions:

- What do I think about the most?
- What do I spend the most time pursuing?
- Where do I spend most of my money?

The answers to questions like these can help us see what our priorities truly are.

Sharing Time: Caught in the River!

One day Jordan was walking home along a trail in the woods after school. His father had said that morning, "Son, come straight home after school today and remember to stay on the trail."

As he was walking, he glanced over to the side. The sight of a sparkling stream caught his eye. Lo and behold, there was a beautiful raft tied to a tree at the side of the stream. The more Jordan looked at that raft, the more he wanted to get in it. So he left the trail and headed for the raft.

Jordan thought to himself, *What could it hurt to just sit in the raft for a few minutes?* So he stepped into the raft. And then, without even thinking and blinded by his excitement, he untied the rope that anchored the raft.

All of a sudden the raft started to move away from the shore and head downstream. As the water picked up speed, the raft went faster and faster. Before long, Jordan was very far from where he was supposed to be.

The world is very much like that. God wants us to walk on a certain path, a certain trail. It is a trail of *righteousness*. But there are things in the world—such as money or possessions—that, if we're not careful, can lure us off the path.

Before long, if we give in to the temptation that distracted us, we can end up very far from where we're supposed to be.

We need to make sure that whatever we come across in the world doesn't pull us away from doing what we know is right. We shouldn't let anything distract us away from Christ.

Confronting the Sin Nature

God tells us not to let our sin nature rule us.

"The acts of the sinful nature are obvious: sexual immorality, impurity and debauchery; idolatry and witchcraft; hatred, discord, jealousy, fits of rage, selfish ambition, dissensions, factions and envy; drunkenness . . . and the like" (Galatians 5:19-21).

The sin nature was not a part of man when God originally created him. Rather, it entered Adam and Eve the moment they disobeyed God and He withdrew His spiritual life from them. Since the time of Adam and Eve, all human beings have been born into the world with a sin nature that rebels against God.

The sin nature and its acts listed in Galatians 5:19-21 greatly hinder our relationship with God. Your child *will* experience many of these things, and, therefore, he or she needs to understand the sin nature's true source. Help your child understand that when we become Christians, the sin nature in us does not go away. It stays with us until we receive our brand-new resurrection bodies in the future. Until that day, the sin nature is ever-present.

The good news is that the *power* of the sin nature to operate in the life of the Christian has been effectively neutralized by virtue of our being united with Christ in His death and sin's defeat. The sin nature has *no right* to reign in the Christian's life any longer, and its power is broken in our lives when we—by faith—accept Jesus' sacrifice (Romans 6:1-14).

Sharing Time: Old Captain, New Captain

This is a story about an awful captain on a ship at sea. This captain is so bad that he is fired from his job as captain, and a new, good captain is brought aboard.

From that moment forward, the people on the ship are supposed to obey only the good captain. But the old, bad captain stays on board. He still goes around trying to give people orders. Nobody is supposed to listen to him. He's no longer the real captain. Sadly, though, some people continue to listen to him and they end up doing bad things.

But people *don't have to listen* to this bad captain. He is no longer the boss. He no longer has any authority over anyone.

In the same way, the old boss or captain of our lives is our sin nature. The sin nature inside us is a bad captain and tries to make us do bad things. But Christ is our new captain. We're now supposed to obey only Him.

Still, the old captain—our sin nature—tries to give us orders to sin. But we don't have to listen. We only have to listen to Christ.

Who are you going to listen to?

Confronting the Devil

God tells us to take a stand against the devil.

"Be self-controlled and alert. Your enemy the devil prowls around like a roaring lion looking for someone to devour" (1 Peter 5:8).

Occasionally your child will hear things about the devil, and he or she may develop incorrect concepts about him. For instance, some children may get the idea that the devil is just a cartoon character—a red figure with horns and a tail. Other children who believe in a real devil may have a distorted picture. They may conclude that the devil is the opposite of God. This means they might think the devil is just as powerful in the realm of evil as God is in the realm of good.

Help your child understand that the devil doesn't have infinite power like God does. There is no comparison between the two in terms of who is stronger and more powerful. The devil has many limitations. God has put Satan on a leash; God has put definite parameters around the devil in regard to how far he can go in his activities. (The book of Job makes this clear.)

The word devil means "liar" or "enemy." The devil is no friend of the Christian. Formerly named "Lucifer," he was originally created as a good angel. But then he became so impressed with himself that he wanted to take God's place. He sinned and rebelled against God. It was then that he became the devil. He has been against God ever since then. One of the reasons Jesus came was to destroy the works of the devil (1 John 3:8).

What does the devil like to do to Christians?

- Satan tempts believers to sin (Ephesians 2:1-3).

- Satan tempts believers to lie (Acts 5:3).

- Satan incites persecutions against believers (Revelation 2:10).

- Satan seeks to plant doubt in the minds of believers (Genesis 3:1-5).

- Satan seeks to foster spiritual pride in the hearts of Christians (1 Timothy 3:6).

Obviously, it is important for every Christian to know what Scripture teaches about this enemy. As you teach your child, it is not necessary that he or she receive a full dose of every dark aspect of the devil. You don't want to spook them.

But, in small doses, help them to increasingly understand who this sinister character is and what he does.

Sharing Time: The Devil's Hook

Have you ever seen anyone go fishing? When people go fishing, they use a hook. But they don't just throw a bare hook out in the water. No fish will want to bite a hook with nothing on it. Instead, the fisherman disguises the hook by putting some bait, like a worm or a grasshopper, on it. The bait tempts the fish to bite. The fish doesn't suspect anything; he thinks it's just food in the water. And when he bites it, the hook suddenly traps him.

The devil does the same kind of thing with us. He tries to tempt us to bite into sin. He goes fishing for Christians to try to make them do things God doesn't like. He puts enticing bait on his hook. So we have to be careful and not be fooled by the devil. He is tricky. We should always be very careful to live like God wants us to. Then we will not be as likely to bite into the devil's hooks.[1]

Our Defense

Fear not, for God has provided everything you need for complete victory over the devil.

"Resist the devil, and he will flee from you" (James 4:7).

Scripture tells us to resist the devil, but how are we to do this? Scripture gives us the answer. God has provided spiritual armor for our defense (Ephesians 6:11-18). Each piece of armor is important and serves its own special purpose. But you and I must choose to put on this armor. God doesn't force us to dress in it.

Without wearing this spiritual armor—the belt of truth, the breastplate of righteousness, the shield of faith, and the like—you and I don't stand a chance against the forces of darkness. But with this armor on, victory is ours.

Wearing this armor means that our lives will be characterized by such things as righteousness, obedience to the will of God, faith in God, and an effective use of the Word of God. Putting on the armor spells DEFEAT for the devil in your life.

Sharing Time: Our Invisible Armor

Whenever there's bad weather outside, we have to wear the right kind of clothing, don't we? If it's raining outside, it's wise to put on a raincoat and a rain hat. That way we don't get wet. If it's freezing cold outside, we put on a big, warm jacket so we don't get cold. We also put on gloves to protect our hands. If there's snow on the ground, we put on boots so snow won't get in our shoes. It's important to wear the right kind of protective clothing when there's bad weather outside.

Did you know that the Bible also talks about protective clothing? The Bible describes it as armor. You've seen pictures of knights with helmets to protect their heads and metal suits, or breastplates, to protect their bodies, right?

The Bible says we need to always keep on our spiritual armor—the belt of truth, the breastplate of righteousness, the shield of faith, and the helmet of salvation. With this armor on, victory over the devil is ours. But how do we wear this spiritual armor?[2]

The Bible tells us that we keep this invisible armor on by living in righteousness, obeying God's will, having faith in God, and reading and applying God's Word. Wearing our spiritual armor means defeat for the devil.

Effective use of the Word of God is especially important for spiritual victory. Jesus used the Word of God to defeat Satan during His wilderness temptations (Matthew 4:1-11).

We must learn to do the same. The greater exposure we have to Scripture, the more the Spirit can use this mighty sword in our lives. If you never read or study your Bible, you leave yourself wide open to defeat and despair.

All of us must be informed and thereby alert to the attacks of Satan (1 Peter 5:8). The apostle Paul says, "We are not ignorant of his schemes" (2 Corinthians 2:11 NASB). We find all the information we need about this enemy and his schemes in the Word of God. Therefore, teach your children to read their Bibles regularly.

We are also instructed to rely on the indwelling Spirit of God, remembering that "the one who is in you is greater than the one who is in the world" (1 John 4:4). Because of our relationship with God, we need not fear the devil.

4

Angels Among Us

"Millions of spiritual creatures walk the earth unseen, both when we wake, and when we sleep: All these with ceaseless praise his works behold both day and night."[1]

—*John Milton*

One biblical truth that never fails to fascinate children is the teaching on angels. I like to call angels "God's invisible helpers." This is a helpful way to describe angels to your children.

Angels are "God's invisible helpers." One of the most important things they do is to watch over us and protect us.

"Are not all angels ministering spirits sent to serve those who will inherit salvation?" (Hebrews 1:14).

"If you make the Most High your dwelling—even the LORD, who is my refuge—then no harm will befall you, no disaster will come near your tent. For he will command his angels concerning you to guard you in all your ways" (Psalm 91:9-11).

The Bible tells us quite a bit about the angels. Here are some interesting facts about angels to share with your child.

Be sure to look up and read together some of the verses that are listed.

- All the angels were instantly created at the same time by God. He spoke the word, and they instantly came into being (Psalm 148:2-5; see also John 1:3).

- The angels were created prior to God's creation of the earth. We know this because Scripture says the angels were singing a song of praise as God created the earth (Job 38:7).

- Since God directly created all the angels at the same time, this means that human beings do not become angels when they die. It is important for your child to understand this, for some Hollywood movies portray humans becoming angels at death (see 1 Corinthians 6:3; 13:1).

- The holy angels live in heaven (Daniel 7:10; Isaiah 6:1-6; Hebrews 12:22). When they are assigned a task by God, they leave heaven, complete their work on earth (or wherever God sends them), and then return to heaven.

- Angels are invisible (Hebrews 1:14). We are thus generally unaware of their activities around us (see 2 Kings 6:17).

- Angels can take on the appearance of human beings when their assigned task calls for it (Genesis 18:1-8; Hebrews 13:2).

- Many angels are described as having wings (Isaiah 6:1-5; Ezekiel 1:6).

- Angels are extremely powerful beings and are described as mighty (Psalm 103:20).

- The holy angels are unreservedly obedient to God (Psalm 103:20).

- Angels are immortal. Once created (Psalm 148:2-5), they never cease to exist (Luke 20:36). They never die.

- The angels are innumerable (Revelation 5:11). Daniel 7:10 makes reference to "ten thousand times ten thousand" angels. This alone adds up to 100,000,000 (one hundred-million) angels.

What the Angels Do for Us

There are many ways that God uses angels to minister to believers. Following are four of the five most important:

1. God sometimes uses angels in answering the prayers of believers. When the early believers prayed for Peter in prison, God sent an angel to break him out of prison. (*Your child will enjoy hearing this story. I recommend that you read Acts 12:3-19 aloud to him or her.*)

2. Angels sometimes serve as God's messengers, bringing announcements, warnings, and other information to the people of God (Genesis 19; Daniel 9; Luke 1:13; Acts 10:3-33).

3. Angels sometimes give people encouragement in times of danger (Acts 27:23,24).

4. Angels are often involved in guarding us against dangers (Psalm 91:9-11).

Sharing Time: God Sent Help!

Angels weren't just created to minister among people in biblical times. They're still here among us.

A Christian missionary in Norway believes an angel assisted him on a dangerous mountain. In attempting to reach families living in his valley, he had to descend a dangerous mountain trail. At one steep, dangerous place he stopped to pray, asking God to protect him with His angels. He safely reached the valley without harm.

At the first cottage, the missionary met a man and his wife who had been watching his descent of the dangerous trail.

"What has become of your companion?" they asked.

"What companion?" the missionary responded.

"The man who was with you," they exclaimed in surprise. "We were watching you as you came down the

204 God's Provision: Power and Protection

mountain, and it really seemed to us that there were two men crossing the mountain together."

"Then," reported the missionary, "I was reminded of my prayer to God for help, and of the word of the Lord in Psalm 34:7, 'The angel of the Lord encampeth round about them that fear him, and delivereth them.' "

Just as the angels protected this man, so the angels protect you too![2]

Sharing Time: I See Jesus!

There's one more very important function of angels—

5. Angels escort believers into heaven at the moment of death (Luke 16:22; Jude 9).

Evangelist Billy Graham said that when his maternal grandmother died, the room seemed to fill with a heavenly light. "She sat up in bed and almost laughingly said, 'I see Jesus. He has His arms outstretched toward me. I see Ben [her husband who had died some years earlier] and I see the angels.' She then slumped over, absent from the body but present with the Lord."[3]

The angels are always there the moment a Christian dies so they can take him or her directly into heaven. Isn't that great?

We should be very thankful to God for sending us His "invisible helpers."

5

Death and the Afterlife

> "There is a land of pure delight,
> Where saints immortal reign;
> Infinite day excludes the night,
> And pleasures banish pain."
> —*"There Is a Land of Pure Delight"(hymn)*

It's natural for your children to have many questions about death and the afterlife. "Why did Uncle Henry have to die?" "Why does anyone have to die?" "Will I go to heaven when I die?" "Is there really a hell?" Admittedly, some of these issues are very difficult to deal with. But we must seek to be biblical in our responses to our children's questions. After all, the Bible is the only source that tells it like it really is on these important issues.

Why Do People Have to Die?

 Death came into the universe when sin came into the universe.

"For the wages of sin is death, but the gift of God is eternal life in Christ Jesus our Lord" (Romans 6:23).

We need to help our kids see the connection between sin and death.

God created Adam and Eve *to live*, not to die. Death is an intruder. It intruded the moment Adam and Eve sinned against God. When Adam and Eve sinned, they were separated from God. This is spiritual death. (The word death actually means "separation." So spiritual death means spiritual separation from God.) Since the time of Adam and Eve, everyone who has been born has been spiritually separated from God. And the direct result of spiritual death is physical death. One leads to the other.

What Happens at the Moment of Death?

 At the moment of death, our spirits depart from our bodies and go straight to heaven.

"We are confident, I say, and would prefer to be away from the body and at home with the Lord" (2 Corinthians 5:8).

"I desire to depart and be with Christ, which is better by far" (Philippians 1:23).

From a biblical perspective, human beings are made up of both a material part (the physical body) and an immaterial part (the soul or spirit). As we noted previously, the New Testament word for "death" literally means separation. When a human being physically dies, his or her spirit departs from the body. This is why Stephen, when he was being put to death by stoning, prayed, "Lord Jesus, receive my spirit" (Acts 7:59). Verses such as this indicate that death for the believer involves his or her spirit immediately going into the presence of the Lord in heaven. Death for the believer is thus an event that leads to a supremely blissful existence.

For the unbeliever, however, dying holds grim prospects. At death the unbeliever's spirit departs from the body and goes not to heaven but to a place of suffering (Luke 16:19-31).

Both believers and unbelievers remain as spirits (in a disembodied state) until the future day of resurrection. And what a glorious day that will be! God will reunite believers' spirits with their resurrected physical bodies. These bodies will be specially suited to dwelling in heaven in the direct presence of God—the perishable will be made imperishable and the mortal will be made immortal (1 Corinthians 15:53). Unbelievers, too, will be resurrected, but they will spend eternity apart from God.

Sharing Time: Going to Heaven

You have a body that you can touch, but the most important part of you is the spirit inside. You have both a body and a spirit.

Look at it this way: You have a hand, and sometimes when it gets cold you put a glove on your hand. Your body is like a glove and your hand is like your spirit. Just like your hand is inside the glove, so your spirit is inside your body.

Now, when a Christian dies, his spirit leaves his body and goes to be with God in heaven.

When the spirit leaves the body, it's kind of like taking your hand out of a glove. The spirit slips out of the body like a hand slips out of a glove, and the spirit goes to be with God in heaven.

In the future, God will resurrect your body and bring it together with your spirit again. Your new body will be like a brand-new glove to put on your hand that will never come off again. Once we get our new resurrection bodies, we'll never be separated from the body again. Isn't that good news?

Will I Go to Heaven When I Die?

All people who believe in Jesus Christ go to heaven.

"I write these things to you who believe in the name of the Son of God so that you may know that you have eternal life" (1 John 5:13).

Here is one way to help your child understand the importance of knowing the Savior:

I can buy a ticket to go on a plane. I can buy a ticket to go on a boat. But no one can buy a ticket to heaven. Going to heaven depends solely on believing in Jesus our Savior. That is God's promise. And God does not lie. When you believe in Jesus, He takes away your sins and gives you the gift of eternal life.

(You might want to review "Evangelizing Your Child" in "Teach Your Children Well.")

Sharing Time: The Map to Heaven

If we were going to take a trip from California to New York, do you think we would need a map? Of course we would. Without a map, we wouldn't know where we were going, would we? But with a map, we'd never get lost.

The Bible is very much like a map, only it doesn't show us how to get to New York. It shows us how to get to heaven. And the most important thing this map—the Bible—tells us is that we need to believe in Jesus. Only those who believe in Jesus go to heaven.

We can go from California to New York using our own efforts. But no amount of effort will get us from earth to heaven. Nobody can do that. The only way to get to heaven is to believe in Jesus!

The Blessing of Heaven

There are no tears in heaven!

"No eye has seen, no ear has heard, no mind has conceived what God has prepared for those who love him" (1 Corinthians 2:9).

Heaven is an abode of resplendent glory. God Himself dwells there. Moreover, in heaven there will be no further death, no further sorrow or tears, and no more pain. That's something to look forward to!

No More Death

The Old Testament promises that in the heavenly state death will be swallowed up forever (Isaiah 25:8). Paul speaks of this same reality as it relates to the future resurrection: "When the perishable has been clothed with the imperishable, and the mortal with immortality, then the saying that is written will come true: 'Death has been swallowed up in victory'" (1 Corinthians 15:54).

What an awesome blessing this is. There will be no more death—no more fatal accidents, no more incurable diseases, no more funeral services, no more final farewells! Death will be gone and done with, never again to be faced by those who dwell in heaven. Life in the eternal city of God will be painless, tearless, and deathless.

Because of what Christ has accomplished for us at the cross, Christ has taken the sting out of death (1 Corinthians 15:55). It no longer has the threat it once did.

Sharing Time: Death Lost Its Stinger!

There was a boy traveling in a car with his father. All of a sudden a bee flew through the open window! The boy was very allergic to bee stings, so he became really frightened.

As he frantically jumped around and tried to avoid the agitated bee, the father calmly reached out, grabbed it, and held it for a moment. When he opened his hand, the bee flew out of his hand.

Then the father said, "Look, son," holding up a hand with an implanted stinger, "his stinger is gone; he can't hurt you any longer."

Just as a bee loses its stinger when it stings someone, so death lost its sting for the Christian when it stung Jesus on the cross. Because of what Jesus did for us, we don't have to be afraid of death any longer.

Sharing Time: The Shadow

Donald Grey Barnhouse had just attended the funeral of his wife. His young child was with him. After leaving the funeral, they were stopped at a traffic light when a large truck sped by, its shadow engulfing them for a brief moment.

Turning to his child, Barnhouse asked, "Tell me, would you rather have been hit by the truck or its shadow?"

The child naturally responded, "Why the shadow, of course."

Barnhouse reflected for a moment, and then said: "That's what happens to us Christians when we die. We are hit by the shadow of death, while those who do not know God are hit with the full force of death."

Because of what Christ accomplished for us at the cross, death no longer carries the pain and horror it once did. It no longer has a stinger.

Serene Rest

Christians in heaven enjoy a sense of serene rest in the presence of Christ. They have no tedious labors to attend to; all is tranquil. The apostle John said, "I heard a voice from heaven say, 'Write: Blessed are the dead who die in the Lord from now on.' 'Yes,' says the Spirit, 'they will rest from their labor . . .'" (Revelation 14:13). This rest will be a comprehensive rest. There will be rest from all toil of the body, from all laborious work, from all the diseases and frailties of the body, from all outward sorrows, from all inward troubles, from the temptations and afflictions of Satan, and from all doubts and fears. *How blessed will be that rest!*

Intimate Fellowship with God and Christ

In heaven we shall see the Lord face to face, as it were, in all His splendor and glory (2 Corinthians 5:6-8; Philippians 1:23). We will gaze upon His countenance and behold His resplendent beauty forever.

In the afterlife there will no longer be intermittent fellowship with the Lord, blighted by sin and defeat. Instead, there will be continuous fellowship. Revelation 21:3 says, "Now the dwelling of God is with men, and he will live with them. They will be his people, and God himself will be with them and be their God." Spiritual death shall never again cause human beings to lose intimate relationship with the Lord because when we enter into glory we will no longer have the sin nature within us. Sin will be banished from our being.

Reunion with Christian Loved Ones

In heaven we will experience a grand reunion with all our Christian loved ones.

> *"The dead in Christ will rise first. After that, we who are still alive and are left will be caught up together with them in the clouds to meet the Lord in the air. And so we will be with the Lord forever"* (1 Thessalonians 4:16,17).

One of the most wonderful aspects of our lives in heaven is that we will be reunited with Christian loved ones. The Thessalonian Christians were apparently very concerned about their Christian loved ones who had died, and they expressed their concern to the apostle Paul.

In 1 Thessalonians 4:13-17, Paul responds and deals with the "dead in Christ" issue. He assures the Thessalonian Christians that there will indeed be a reunion in heaven. And yes, believers will recognize their loved ones in the eternal state (see 2 Samuel 12:23; Matthew 17:1-8; Luke 16:19-31).

Be sure that your children understand this glorious truth.

Sharing Time: A Joyful Reunion

Do you remember the story I told you earlier about Donald Grey Barnhouse? His wife had died, and he and his little boy went to her funeral.

Since then Mr. Barnhouse has died, too. And you know what? He is together right now with his wife in heaven. How joyful Mr. Barnhouse must have been when he entered heaven after his death and saw his wife's face again. They had a reunion. And one day, their son, who is now a grown-up, will have a reunion with them in heaven, too!

When we die, we'll be together with all our Christian loved ones in heaven. Isn't that great?

What About Unbelievers?

Those who die having rejected Jesus Christ as Savior will not go to heaven, but to hell.

> *"Then he will say to those on his left, 'Depart from me, you who are cursed, into the eternal fire prepared for the devil and his angels' "* (Matthew 25:41).

The Scriptures say that hell is a real place. Hell, in the Bible, is portrayed as a place of horror (Revelation 20:10), weeping (Matthew 8:12), and punishment (Matthew 25:46). It is also described as the lake of fire (Revelation 20:14).

Emphasize to your child that God doesn't want to send anyone to hell. That's why He sent Jesus—to pay the penalty for our sins by dying on the cross. But, unfortunately, not all people are willing to admit that they sin and need to ask for forgiveness. They don't accept the payment of Jesus' death for them. So God lets them experience the results of their choice.

C.S. Lewis once said that in the end there are two groups of people. One group of people says to God, "Thy will be done." These are those who have placed their faith in Jesus Christ and will live forever with God in heaven. The second group of people are those to whom God says, sadly, "*Thy* will be done!" These are the people who have rejected Jesus Christ and will spend eternity apart from Him.

Let your child know that the reality of hell should motivate each of us to share the good news of the gospel to as many people as we can. Also reassure them that *we don't have to worry* about hell because we have trusted in Jesus for our salvation (see John 3:16,17).

The Resurrection Body

God has promised to give us a resurrection body that will last forever.

> *"When the perishable has been clothed with the imperishable, and the mortal with immortality, then the saying that is written will come true: 'Death has been swallowed up in victory'"* (1 Corinthians 15:54).

Our present bodies are characterized by weakness. The seeds of disease and death are ever upon us. From the moment we are born, the "outward man is decaying" (2 Corinthians 4:16). Vitality decreases, illness comes, and then old age follows. In old age, we may become utterly incapacitated, not able to move around and do the simplest of tasks. And all of us eventually die. It's just a matter of time.

Our new resurrection bodies, however, will be raised imperishable (1 Corinthians 15:42,43). All liability to disease and death will be forever gone. Never again will we have to worry about infections or passing away. Never again will we tire, become weak, or become incapacitated.

Sharing Time: The Forever Tent

(You might want to read 2 Corinthians 5:1-9 for more details on this great analogy.)

The body we now have is a temporary body. After we get to heaven, the Bible says we will receive a resurrection body that will never die!

Your body is kind of like a tent. Have you ever slept in a tent? It's a fun thing to do. Of course, a tent is not made to last very long. A strong wind could even blow it down. And it's not nearly as strong as a building. If somebody ran into the tent, the tent would probably fall down. So it's not very strong. In the same way, our present bodies are not really strong—and that's why people die. Their bodies "fall down" in death.

But our future resurrection body will be like a strong and powerful building. Nobody can knock it down—even a strong wind can't knock it down. It will be a body that lasts forever.

Developing an Eternal Perspective

Live your life on earth with eternity on your mind.

"Set your minds on things above, not on earthly things" (Colossians 3:2).

Our true significance comes not from attaining a certain status and the accumulation of earthly possessions, but from our relationship with Jesus Christ. After all, we will not take our position or wealth with us into the next life.

The incredible glory of the afterlife should motivate each of us to live faithfully during our relatively short time on earth. When difficult times come, we must remember that we are but pilgrims on our way to another land—to heaven, where Christ Himself dwells (Philippians 3:20).

6

Spiritual Growth

"Spiritual maturity—the quiet confidence
that God is in control."[1]
— *Charles Swindoll*

The whole issue of growing in spirituality is an important one for our children. Too often, parents wait until later
childhood before they start to take their kids' spiritual growth
very seriously. This is not as it should be. Spiritual growth
should start early—as early as your children are able.

Unlike measuring physical or emotional growth, spiritual development is not an easy area to measure in the lives
of our children. One thing to keep in mind in regard to our
children's spiritual progress is that it will not follow a straight
line. Just like us, our children will have ups and downs; there
will be peaks and valleys. This is natural. Allow them room
to grow. Understand that there will be phases they go through
as they mature spiritually. And no matter what, whether they
are on a peak or in a valley, make sure they feel loved, accepted, and appreciated.

Now, let's discuss some specifics that can contribute to
your child's spiritual growth.

Be an Example

The experts say that those families that are being most
effective in helping their children grow spiritually are those

that make faith relevant to living. They make faith come alive in everyday ways. One way to do this is to plan daily activities that will help your children see the reality of a faith in God. This way there is steady progress in the spiritual development of the child.

Here is one of many possible examples: If you get sick or are having a bad day, ask your child to pray for you. Likewise, if your child is sick or is having a bad day, sit down and pray for him or her. Our children will learn from our example. John Maxwell tells us that—

> we should never underestimate the power of our example on our children. We teach what we know, but we reproduce what we are. Much of what we do today was modeled for us by our parents. For example, without my mother knowing it, I often listened outside my parents' room as she prayed. I learned a lot from that, and it has helped me to be intimate with God in my prayers as an adult.[2]

Learning to Love God

 A key measuring stick of spiritual growth is your personal love for God.

"Love the Lord your God with all your heart and with all your soul and with all your mind" (Matthew 22:37).

Emphasize to your children that when someone truly loves God with all his heart, it has an effect on his behavior and mindset. For example:

- People who love God talk to Him a lot in prayer.

- People who love God seek to obey His will.

- People who love God turn to Him whenever they get frightened.

- People who love God spend time reading the Bible.

Sharing Time: Best Friends

During the summer Arnie, along with his mom and dad, went to visit Grandpa for a week. It was such a fun time. Arnie really liked to be with his Grandpa.

One day Arnie was talking to Grandpa and said, "Grandpa, when you come to our house, I want you to meet my friend Joe. We hang out together a lot and play and talk. You'll like him, Grandpa. He's my best buddy!"

Grandpa said, "I would really like that. He sounds like a fun kind of guy."

"Yes, he is," said Arnie. "Grandpa, who's your best friend?"

"My best friend is the Lord," Grandpa replied.

"Is that why you talk to talk to Him so much and read the Bible so often?"

"That's right," Grandpa said. "When you love someone, you like to spend a lot of time with that person. You like to talk to that person. You like to do things that your friend likes for you to do. And you know what else? God wants us to love Him more than anyone else. That means it's important for us to spend time with Him and talk to Him in prayer. It also means we should seek to do the things He wants us to do."

"Wow, I want to love God like that, too!" Arnie said.

Learning to Love Others

The second greatest commandment is to love others as we love ourselves.

"Love your neighbor as yourself" (Matthew 22:39).

Help your children to understand that if they truly love others as they love themselves—as Scripture commands— this will have an effect on their behavior and their mindset. For example:

- They will be sensitive to the feelings of other children.

- They will share their belongings with others.

- They will pray for others.

Sharing Time: A Lesson from a Doll

Becky was so excited because her friend Lisa was coming over to eat lunch and to play. As she was waiting for Lisa to show up, Becky played in her room with a little doll she loved.

"Are you cold?" Becky asked her doll. "Here, you can have my blanket to keep you warm!"

"Are you hungry?" Becky asked her doll. "Here are some cookies for you to eat!"

"Are you tired?" Becky asked her doll. "Here, you can lay down in my bed to rest!"

"What would you like to do now?" Becky asked her doll. "We can do anything you like."

Then the doorbell rang—Lisa was finally here. So Becky ran downstairs to be with her friend.

After lunch, Becky's mom offered the girls a popsicle for dessert. "We have grape popsicles, orange ones, and a red one. Pick out your flavor."

Lisa wanted the red one, but Becky wanted it too and she got her hands on it first. So Lisa chose an orange one instead.

Becky and Lisa then talked about what they wanted to do next. Lisa wanted to go outside and play jump rope. But Becky wanted to go to her room and play "dress up." Becky argued and got her way.

Once they were in Becky's room, they started to play "dress up."

Lisa asked, "Can I put on the princess crown that's on your dresser?"

"No," Becky said, "I want to wear that. You can wear something else." This made Lisa a little sad.

Just then, Becky's mom said, "Becky, may I talk to you for a moment here in the hall?"

"You know," her mom said, "just a while ago I saw you treat your doll with such love. You were putting her needs first. You need to do the same thing with real people like Lisa. After all, the Bible says we should love others as we love ourselves."

Becky knew that was true, and she did want to be a good friend to Lisa. So she went back into her room, took the princess crown off her head, and put it on Lisa's head. She smiled and said to Lisa, "You look pretty in that crown!"

Becky then asked Lisa, "What would *you* like to do now? If you like, we can go play jump rope outside."

Teach Your Child to Pray

We can pray to God about anything.

"Do not be anxious about anything, but in everything, by prayer and petition, with thanksgiving, present your requests to God" (Philippians 4:6).

I remember when I was young and my sister was given a plastic doll. As she played with it day in and day out, one of the arms ended up being broken off. My sister promptly went to my dad to fix it. And my dad was glad to do it. But my sister didn't want to let go of the doll. She wanted to keep holding on to it. This effectively prevented my father from fixing it.

Soon after, another arm of the doll broke off. Again she went to my dad to fix it, but she didn't want to let go of it. Again my father was prevented from fixing it.

Pretty soon both of the legs popped off, too. By this time my sister was getting desperate. So, finally mustering all her strength of will, she surrendered the broken mess to my father. Within minutes my dad had the doll reassembled as good as new.

This illustrates the way you and I often are with God. Sometimes we go to God in prayer about a matter, but we really don't entrust the entire situation to Him. We hold on to it, and fret about it, and try to solve the problem in our own strength. It's often when things get desperately bad that we finally turn to God and release everything into His care. How much wiser it would be to turn every problem over to God as each problem arises.

The Scriptures instruct us not to be anxious but to entrust everything to God in prayer (Philippians 4:6,7). No problem is too small or too big to put in His care. Like a friend, He is always there to listen to our prayers. He never shuts us out.

God certainly hears the prayers of children, and *He answers them.* I read a story told by child evangelism expert Eric Stuyck that perfectly illustrates this:

> I was told of a five-year old named David. David's parents had adopted him after having given up hope of having their own children (something they both wanted very badly). Knowing this, David continually brought the matter up as a prayer request in the class at the Christian school where he, as a believer, was being taught to pray. He asked that they would pray that his mother get pregnant.
>
> The teacher brought this to the attention of David's mother (who happened to be the school nurse) who in turn asked her husband to have a talk with David. His response to her was to let it alone so he could learn that sometimes God answers "no."
>
> Within the year, David's mother was pregnant. After her first baby, she was soon pregnant again! (I guess David hadn't stopped praying.)
>
> This time his mother *did* sit him down to have a talk with him about all this praying. But David looked up at her and said, "But Mom, you shouldn't be surprised. I asked for four!"
>
> The last I heard, they had only had two. I guess David needed to learn that sometimes God answers, "Enough."[3]

Of course, there will inevitably come a time when your child will claim that God didn't answer his or her prayer. When that happens, discuss the matter. Inform them that God *always* hears our prayers, but He doesn't always say yes to our requests (1 John 5:14). Sometimes He says no. Sometimes He says wait. Like a good parent, God doesn't always give us what we want but He gives us what we need. God always has our best interests at heart.

Please encourage your children to pray. Tell them that God *delights* to answer their prayers. Teach your children to pray, and be prepared to see results!

Sharing Time: God Hears You!

Do you know what a walkie-talkie is? If we both have one, we can walk far away from each other and still talk to each other! We only have to press the button on the walkie-talkie. I can be in the house and you can be in the yard, and we can still talk to each other.

Did you know we can talk to God whenever we want—and *we don't need to have a walkie-talkie*? That's right. We can talk to God in prayer. And He *always* hears us, no matter where we are. There's no place you can go where God won't hear you when you pray.[4]

I like to talk to God every day in prayer. Do you mind if we pray right now? (*Lead your child in a prayer of your choosing.*)

Pray *for* Your Kids

Besides teaching our kids *how* to pray, it is critically important that we also *pray for* them. No doubt you already do this, but it never hurts to be reminded about the kinds of things we ought to be praying for in regard to our children. Joe White has assembled this excellent list:

- Pray that nothing will hinder your children from accepting Christ as their personal Savior early in life (see Matthew 18:6; 19:14).

- Pray that your children will learn to know their God, the true and living God, and will have a deep desire to do His will for their lives (see Psalm 119:27,30,34,35).

- Pray that as your children hear stories from the Bible, a genuine love for God and His Word will become such a part of their lives that it will be the basis for all their decision-making throughout life (see Psalm 71:17; Ecclesiastes 12:1; 2 Timothy 3:15).

- Pray that your children will develop a keen sense of what's right and wrong—that they will truly abhor evil and cling to that which is good (see Psalm 51:10; 139:23,24; Romans 12:9).

- Pray that your kids will increase in wisdom mentally, in stature physically, and in favor with God spiritually and man socially (see Luke 2:52).

- Pray that your children will develop a thankful heart and a fine, confident mental attitude (see Psalm 126:2,3; Romans 8:31).

- Pray that God will protect your kids from Satan and his wiles in every area of their lives (see Psalm 121:8; John 17:15).

- Pray that God will destroy the "enemies" in your children's lives, whatever they may be—weaknesses, lying, selfishness, disobedience, and so on (see Psalm 120:2; Philippians 2:4).

- Pray that God will make your kids successful in the work He has planned for them to do (see Psalm 118:25; 139:9,10).

- Pray that your children will have a strong sense of belonging to His family (see Psalm 133; Colossians 3:12-14).

- Pray that your kids will respect those in authority over them (see Romans 13:1; Ephesians 6:1-4).

- Pray that their entire lives will be a testimony of the greatness and love of Jesus Christ (see Philippians 2:15-16; 1 Thessalonians 5:23).[5]

When Life Throws a Punch

God sometimes allows us to go through tough times to make us better people.

"We also rejoice in our sufferings, because we know that suffering produces perseverance; perseverance, character; and character, hope" (Romans 5:3,4).

In Romans 5:3,4, the apostle Paul is saying that suffering can actually be good for us. We need to remember that when we encounter tough times. God may be allowing us to go through those circumstances in order to make us grow. God uses such circumstances to take the rough edges off our character.

Sharing Time: A Lesson from Popcorn

Do you like popcorn? I sure do.

When you put popcorn in the microwave oven, heat is applied to the popcorn kernels. This makes each of the kernels pop. The heat brings about a change in the kernel. It turns it into a delicious, fluffy, white, crunchy treat. Without the heat, the popcorn would remain just a hard kernel. Not a very good snack!

Sometimes we encounter "heat" in daily life—that is, we encounter tough times. You might have a bad day at school. Or maybe you might lose one of your favorite toys.

These tough times can bring about a positive change in our character. That's the way God planned it. Our suffering produces perseverance and hope. These are good qualities to have.

For example, if you have a bad day at school, God might use that to teach you to have faith. If you lose a toy, God might use that to teach you patience as you look for the toy.

The Eye of Faith

You can trust God. He'll never let you down.

"Now faith is being sure of what we hope for and certain of what we do not see" (Hebrews 11:1).

Do you remember the story of Elisha in 2 Kings 6:8-23? Elisha found himself in a situation where he was completely surrounded by enemy troops, yet he remained calm and relaxed. His servant, however, must have been climbing the walls at the sight of this hostile army with vicious-looking warriors and innumerable battle-chariots on every side. [I envision this servant as being kind of like a Don Knotts character.]

Undaunted, Elisha said to him: "Don't be afraid.... Those who are with us are more than those who are with them" (2 Kings 6:16). Elisha then prayed to God, "'O LORD, open his eyes so he may see.' Then the LORD opened the servant's eyes, and he looked and saw the hills full of horses and chariots of fire all around Elisha" (2 Kings 6:17). God was protecting Elisha and his servant with a whole army of magnificent angels!

The reason Elisha never got worried was because he was sure of what he hoped for and certain of what he did not see. The eye of faith recognizes that God acts on our behalf even when we don't perceive it with our physical senses. Be sure to share this biblical story with your child because we must teach our children to have that eye of faith.

Helping Your Child Discover His S-H-A-P-E

In many ways, a person's "shape" goes a long way in determining his ministry throughout life. Now, of course, a young child is still in the process of having his shape formed, as we all are to some degree throughout our lives. But I believe that in their later childhood and teen years our kids can and should begin to discover their "shape" and begin involving themselves in ministry at church.

- Job said to God, "Your hands shaped me and made me" (Job 10:8).

- The psalmist said, "I praise you because I am fearfully and wonderfully made; your works are wonderful, I know that full well. My frame was not hidden from you when I was made in the secret place. When I was woven together in the depths of the earth, your eyes saw my unformed body" (Psalm 139:14-16).

My pastor, Rick Warren, has developed an acronym—SHAPE—that is of great benefit toward discovering a person's God-intended place of ministry in the body of Christ.[6]

S – *Spiritual Gifts:* God has given every single Christian one or more spiritual gifts (1 Corinthians 7:7).

H – *Heart:* Every Christian has different tastes and likes and they come to love different things (cf. Revelation 17:17; Philippians 2:13). Not every person has the "heart" to do the same things.

A – *Abilities:* God has given each one of us natural abilities and talents (cf. 1 Corinthians 12:6; Exodus 31:3; 2 Corinthians 3:5).

P – *Personality:* People have different personalities. Some people have the personality to do a particular thing, while others do not. We should do that which is suited to our particular personality (cf. 1 Corinthians 2:11).

E – *Experiences:* Each one of us has had a variety of experiences: spiritual (Hebrews 5:12-14), painful (Proverbs 20:30), educational (Proverbs 4:13), and ministry (2 Corinthians 9:13).

In view of these factors, one way to help our kids in later childhood to discover what kind of ministry they'd be good at would be to determine:

- What are they gifted to do? (**Spiritual gifts**)

- What do they love to do? (Heart)

- What natural talents and skills do they have? (Abilities)

- Where does their personality best suit them to serve? (Personality)

- What kinds of experiences have they had? (Experiences)

As they grow up, these are questions our children will have to answer for themselves. But you can begin providing guidance for them so they'll be headed in the right direction. We need to help our children discover their place of ministry according to their God-given "shape."

Survival Training:
Learning What to Avoid

1

Cult-Proofing Your Kids

"This is the most crucial decade in history. Designer, à la carte religion flourishes as traditional Christianity is undermined by counterfeits."[1]

— George Gallup

Beware of groups that claim to be Christian but deny key doctrines of Christianity.

"Watch out for false prophets. They come to you in sheep's clothing, but inwardly they are ferocious wolves" (Matthew 7:15).

It is important that your child come to understand that there are counterfeit religious groups called cults. These groups typically claim to be Christian, but they're not because they deny one or more of the essential doctrines of the Christian faith.

In a cult we typically find an emphasis on new revelation from God, a denial of the sole authority of the Bible, a distorted view of God and Jesus, and a denial of salvation by grace. These are red flags you will want your kids to be aware of.

New Revelation

Many cult leaders claim to have a direct pipeline to God. The teachings of the cult often change, and, hence, they need new so-called "revelations" to justify such changes. Mormons, for example, once excluded African-Americans from their priesthood. When social pressure was exerted against the Church of Jesus Christ of Latter-day Saints for this blatant form of racism, the Mormon president received a new "revelation" reversing the previous decree.

Denial of the Sole Authority of the Bible

Many cults deny the sole authority of the Bible. They often supplement the Bible with another book by the cult leader.

- Christian Scientists elevate Mary Baker Eddy's book *Science and Health* to supreme authority.

- Reverend Moon placed his book *The Divine Principle* in authority over all his followers.

- Mormons believe the Book of Mormon is higher Scripture than the Bible.

A Distorted View of God and Jesus

Cults typically put forth a distorted view of God and Jesus. They have a different God and a different Jesus from that of the Bible.

- Jehovah's Witnesses say Jesus was a lesser god than God the Father.

- Mormons say Jesus was the spirit-brother of Lucifer.

- Baha'is say Jesus was just one of many prophets of God.

Denial of Salvation by Grace

Cults typically deny salvation by grace, thus distorting the purity of the gospel.

- Mormons, for example, emphasize that attaining perfection is necessary for salvation.

- Jehovah's Witnesses emphasize the importance of distributing Watchtower literature door-to-door as a part of "working out" their salvation.

- Herbert W. Armstrong said that the idea that works are not required for salvation is rooted in Satan.

Beware!

From the brief survey above, it is clear that cults typically deny one or more of the essential doctrines of Christianity. Help your children recognize these danger signals. Teach them well.

Sharing Time: Pretend Christians

One day Jerry was with his dad, who worked in the orchards as a fieldhand. It was a hot sunny afternoon, and Jerry was famished. When he saw a tree laden with peaches, he scurried over to it. There was one peach that was within his reach. He quickly noticed the red blush on its orange skin, and he knew it was ripe for his enjoyment. He touched it, and it felt soft and round in his hand. He wanted it.

Just as Jerry was about to bite into it, his dad grabbed it out of his hand. His dad looked at it closely, and then he broke it open. A slimy worm was crawling around the core of the peach. The peach looked good on the outside, but on the inside it was not good.[2]

Jesus also warned us about things that look good on the outside but aren't good on the inside. He said, "Watch out for false prophets. They come to you in sheep's clothing, but inwardly they are ferocious wolves" (Matthew 7:15).

False prophets lead groups that claim to be Christian, but they're not really. They are called "cults." Cults are not Christian because they say things that aren't true about Jesus and God. Some say there are other books from God besides the Bible—but that's not true.

We have to be careful about cults. They're very deceptive because they look good on the outside, but they're not good on the inside.

2

Refuting Reincarnation

> "Reincarnation is like show business. You
> just keep doing it until you get it right."[1]
> —*Shirley MacLaine*

 Reincarnation is the false view that when a
person dies he comes back to earth born as
someone new.

*"Man is destined to die once, and after that to face
judgment"* (Hebrews 9:27).

With the plethora of eastern religions growing in
America, your child will inevitably be introduced to the doctrine of reincarnation at some point. *Warn them!*

Reincarnation involves the idea that one is born again
and again and again. With each new birth, one allegedly gets
better and better until one day, one can break away from reincarnation altogether and attain union with pure bliss (Nir-
vana).

Reincarnation goes against the whole of Scripture. First, while
the doctrine of reincarnation teaches that people die over and
over again until they reach perfection, the Bible teaches that
it is appointed for men to die *once*, and after that comes the
judgment. Each human being lives once as a mortal on earth,
dies once, and then faces judgment.

Second, Jesus taught that people decide their eternal des-
tiny in a *single* lifetime (Matthew 25:46). This is precisely why

the apostle Paul emphasized that "now is the day of salvation" (2 Corinthians 6:2).

Third, Scripture indicates that at the moment of death believers go into the presence of the Lord (2 Corinthians 5:8) and unbelievers go to a place of suffering (Luke 16:19-31) and not into another body.

Sharing Time: What Happens When We Die?

Alice went up to her mommy and asked, "Mom, what is reincarnation?"

"Where did you hear that word, Alice?" her mom responded.

"I heard it on cartoons this morning when I was watching TV," Alice said. "The person in the cartoon said he was a great warrior in a past life. What does that mean?"

"Reincarnation is not true, Alice," her mom said. "There are many people who believe in it, but the Bible says it's not true. Reincarnation is the idea that when a person dies they are then born into another human body. But do you remember what Jesus said happens when we die?"

"Yes, Mom," Alice said. "Jesus said that if we're Christians we go to heaven when we die."

"That's right," her mom said. "We're not born on earth again in another body."

Alice's mom reflected for a moment, and then said, "Alice, I'm so glad you asked me about this. When we hear things that we're not sure about—like reincarnation—we should always go to the Bible to check it out, right?"

"Right, Mom!" Alice responded.

3

Unmasking Eastern Meditation

"The lost art of the twentieth century is
meditation."[1]

—*Charles Swindoll*

 Christians should meditate only on the Bible.

*"Do not let this Book of the Law depart from your
mouth; meditate on it day and night, so that you
may be careful to do everything written in it"*
(Joshua 1:8).

There are many dangers in practicing Eastern forms of
meditation. In these forms of meditation, one is taught to
empty the mind of all thoughts in order to achieve a supernatural experience. Eastern meditation is entirely subjective
and experiential in nature. Moreover, Eastern forms of meditation may involve "focusing" or "centering" on various objects drawn from Hinduism or Buddhism. This ultimately
involves losing one's personhood and individuality, and
merging with the "One." This is far removed from the ob-
jective form of meditation found in the Bible.

Biblical meditation, by contrast, involves pondering
God's Word and His faithfulness (Joshua 1:8; Psalm 119:148).
There is obviously a big difference between emptying one's
mind to meditate *on nothing* and filling one's mind with the
Word of God to meditate *on the living God.* David meditated
on God's Word (Psalm 48:9; 77:12; 143:5). His purpose was

spiritual fellowship with God, not a mystical union with Brahman or the Tao of Eastern religions. The two forms of meditation are entirely different.

Many words in the Hebrew language are rich with nuances of meaning that sometimes fail to come across in English translations. The Hebrew term for "meditation" is such a word. In different contexts, "meditate" can mean *to utter, imagine, speak, roar, mutter, meditate,* and *muse.* For example, this Hebrew word in Isaiah 31:4 is translated to express the roar of a lion. Similarly, it is used in Isaiah 38:14 in reference to the sound of the mourning of doves. In both cases, the idea seems to be that *outward expression is an outgrowth of strong inner emotions and thoughts.*

The term seems to carry the basic idea of "murmuring." It portrays a person who is very deep in thought, mumbling with his lips as though talking to himself. It is as if strong feelings build up in the innermost depths of his soul, and the pressure is finally released (like steam) in verbal expression. When David meditated on God's Word, he concentrated so intensely that he no doubt murmured with his lips as he read.

Sharing Time: Meditating God's Way

You know what a hammer is, right? It's just a tool. And like any tool, you can use a hammer in the right way and you can use a hammer in the wrong way.

We use a hammer in the right way when we use it to build a house. But we use a hammer the wrong way when we swing it carelessly—possibly breaking something or, worse yet, hitting someone! We should use a hammer *only* in the right way.

Meditation is the same way. It can be used in the right way or in the wrong way. Some people use meditation to try to make their minds think about nothing. They try to empty their minds. That's the wrong way to use meditation. God doesn't want us to sit and think about nothing. God doesn't want our minds to be empty.

Other people use meditation to think about God's Word. They make their minds *fill up* with the Bible. That's the right use of meditation. God likes us to think about His Word and keep it in our minds. When we meditate, we should always be careful to do it God's way!

4

Panning Pantheism

"God is exalted far above the created universe, so far above that human thought cannot imagine it."[1]

—*A.W. Tozer*

God is eternally distinct from *(and above)* His creation.

"The heavens, even the highest heaven, cannot contain you. How much less this temple I have built!" (1 Kings 8:27).

Pantheism is the view that "all is God and God is all." This is the view of God set forth in Eastern religions such as Hinduism. A pantheistic view of God is completely incompatible with Christianity. As our children grow older it is important that they understand this incompatibility, for they will surely encounter pantheism through the influence of the New Age movement.

Following are three of the more critical problems with a pantheistic view of God.

1. In pantheism all distinctions between creation (which is finite) and the Creator (who is infinite) are ultimately destroyed. This means there is really no distinction between God, John, Sally, Fred, and Susan. If all is God, then such personal distinctions are impossible. But

because John, Sally, Fred, and Susan *are* distinct from each other (and from God), pantheism cannot be true (see Ecclesiastes 5:2; Numbers 23:19).

2. A pantheistic view of God cannot adequately deal with the existence of evil in the world. If God is the essence of *all* life forms in creation, then one must conclude that both good *and* evil stem from one and the same essence (God). Contrary to this, the God of the Bible is light, and "in Him there is no darkness at all" (1 John 1:5; see also Habakkuk 1:13; Matthew 5:48).

3. The God of pantheism is an *impersonal* force, not a personal Being with whom relationships can be established. The biblical concept of God, by contrast, involves a loving Father unto whom believers may cry, "Abba" (which loosely means "Daddy") (Mark 14:36; Romans 8:15; Galatians 4:6).

Sharing Time: Can We Touch God?

Do you think the chair you're sitting in is God? Of course not.

Do you think the food you eat for breakfast, lunch, and dinner is God? Of course not.

Do you think the clothes you are wearing are God? No way.

Some people wrongly believe that everything you can see and touch is God, but that's not true, is it? That's not what the Bible teaches.

The Bible says that God is the Creator, and He made all the things you can see and touch. So we shouldn't get confused and start thinking that our chair and food and clothes are God. That wouldn't make sense, would it?

Now, here's something to think about: Your chair and food and clothes (and everything else) are not God. But God is present with us no matter where we go in the world. Simply because God is present with us wherever we go, though, doesn't mean that God is the chair and the food and the clothes and all the other stuff we see. God is an invisible spirit. We can't see Him, but He is always with us.

5

Curbing the Craving to Be God

"Of two things we can be certain: there is a God and you are not him."

—*Anonymous*

Man is not God nor will he *ever* become God.

"Is there any God besides me? No, there is no other Rock; I know not one" (Isaiah 44:8).

"Before me no god was formed, nor will there be one after me" (Isaiah 43:10).

The perverted desire for godhood has a long history in the universe. If it is correct that Isaiah 14:12-14 and Ezekiel 28:12-19 refer to the fall of Lucifer (and there is good reason to believe this), then it seems that this was the beginning of the desire for godhood in the universe.

Lucifer was originally created as the most magnificent of angels. But then an unholy desire entered his heart. His sinful yearning is summed up in the statement, "I will make myself like the Most High" (Isaiah 14:14). Lucifer wanted to take God's place. But the *only true God* cast the self-inflated Lucifer from His holy presence.

In the Garden of Eden, this fallen angel sought to tempt Eve to eat the forbidden fruit. He enticed her by saying, "God knows that in the day you eat from it your eyes will be opened, and *you will be like God,* knowing good and evil" (Genesis 3:5 NASB, emphasis added). The fall of man was the result of this encounter. But man—to the present day—continues yearning to be God.

In total antithesis to the idea that man is a god (or can become god), the biblical view is that no one on earth comes even remotely close to God's greatness and majesty. Do you recall the message God instructed Moses to pass on to Pharaoh regarding the ten plagues? "I will send all My plagues on you and your servants and your people, *so that you may know that there is no one like Me in all the earth*" (Exodus 9:14 NASB, emphasis added).

When it is realized that these words were spoken to a man who was himself considered a god by his people (the Pharaoh was thought to be the incarnation of the Egyptian sun god, Re, and was considered a god in his own right), these words of the one true God become extremely relevant to the current New Age claim that human beings are divine. God's response to such claims is that "there is no one like Me in all the earth."

If it were true (hypothetically) that human beings are gods, then one would expect them to display qualities similar to those known to be true of God. However, when one compares the attributes of humankind with those of God, we find more than ample testimony for the truth of Paul's statement in Romans 3:23 that human beings "fall short of the glory of God." Consider the following:

- God is all-knowing (Isaiah 40:13,14); man is limited in knowledge (Job 38:4)

- God is all-powerful (Revelation 19:6); man is weak (Hebrews 4:15)

- God is everywhere-present (Psalm 139:7-12); man is confined to a single space at a time (John 1:50)

- God is holy (1 John 1:5); even man's righteous deeds are as filthy garments before God (Isaiah 64:6)

- God is eternal (Psalm 90:2); man was created at a point in time (Genesis 1:1,26,27)

- God is truth (John 14:6); man's heart is deceitful above all else (Jeremiah 17:9)

- God is characterized by justice (Acts 17:31); man is lawless (1 John 3:4; see also Romans 3:23)

- God is love (Ephesians 2:4,5); man is plagued with numerous vices like jealousy and strife (1 Corinthians 3:3).

Our children will certainly encounter New Agers as they grow up. We must therefore make sure that they thoroughly understand the scriptural view that becoming God is never an option for a human being.

Sharing Time: Silly People

There was once a very righteous man who was sharing the gospel and doing the work of ministry in a particular city. God used this man to perform an incredible miracle that brought healing to a crippled man. And do you know what happened next?

Some of the people of that city thought this man was God. Isn't that silly? These people thought he was a god and were preparing to worship him as a god.

When this righteous man realized what they were doing, he ran out among them and shouted to them to stop. He told them he was just an ordinary man like they were. This man knew that no human being can become a god.

This man was the apostle Paul (see Acts 14). We read about him throughout the New Testament.

Today there are people who still believe that human beings can become gods. But we know this isn't true, don't we?

The Bible says there is only one true God. Human beings can never become a God.*

Becoming Godly

Although human beings can never become God, Christians are called to become more and more *godly*. We can do this in the sense that as we walk in dependence upon the Holy Spirit, we reflect God's righteousness more and more through our behavior. This is godly living. It is not in any sense becoming "divine."

---

* If your child asks how this relates to Jesus, point out that Jesus wasn't a man who became a god, but was rather God who became a man. Jesus has always been God!

6

Avoiding Astrology

"Esau and Jacob were born of the same
father and mother, at the same time, and
under the same planets, but their nature
was wholly different. You would per-
suade me that astrology is a true science!"[1]
—*Martin Luther to Melanchthon*

God condemns astrology.

*"Surely they [astrologers] are like stubble; the fire
will burn them up. They cannot even save themselves from the power of the flame. . . . Each of them
goes on in his error; there is not one that can save
you" (Isaiah 47:14,15).*

Astrology can be traced back to the religious practices of
ancient Mesopotamia, Assyria, and Egypt. It is a form of div-
ination—an attempt to seek counsel or knowledge by oc-
cultic means—that was popular among the people of those
nations.

Some people believe that our lives are affected by the
movement of the stars in the sky. They read horoscopes in
the daily newspaper because they think they can receive direction for living by reading about the stars and planets. This
is sheer folly. Astrology—*and* reading horoscopes—is strictly
off-limits for the Christian.

Astrology is flatly condemned by God in Scripture. In Isaiah 47, for example, we find a strong denunciation of astrologers and their craft. Verse 15 explicitly states that "each of them goes on in his error," and "there is not one that can save you." The book of Daniel confirms that astrologers lack true discernment. The only source of accurate revelation is God Almighty (Daniel 2:1-28, especially verses 2,10,27, and 28).

God created the stars. They have no intrinsic power to affect human destinies. When we need help, we should pray for God's guidance (James 1:5) and read the Bible. God's Word can act as a lamp unto our feet (Psalm 119:105).

Sharing Time: Wolf in Sheep's Clothing

Kelly, Lindsay, and Alyssa were walking around in the mall on Friday after school. They went into a popular bookstore. Lindsay's eye caught sight of a sign in the store pointing to books on astrology. She quickly walked over to that section and called Kelly and Alyssa to follow.

They saw books on how astrology can affect your love life, your popularity, making money, what lies in your future, and much more. There were all kinds of books on astrology.

Lindsay said to Kelly and Alyssa, "Hey, what are your signs? Let's see what these books say about us."

Kelly immediately backed up and said, "Whoa! Wait a minute! I don't want to do that. Our youth group leader at church said we need to stay away from all this astrology stuff. He said we shouldn't look to the stars for guidance, but we should instead look to the God who *made* the stars for guidance."

"Oh, there's no harm in it," Lindsay replied. "It's all in good fun. Nobody really believes this stuff. Come on, what's your sign?"

"No, really, I don't want to!" Kelly insisted. "Our youth group leader even had us memorize a verse in the book of Isaiah where God condemns astrology. In this case, what appears to be harmless may be a wolf in sheep's clothing."

"Besides," Kelly said, "I already know what's in my immediate future. I'm going for an ice-cream cone. Let's go!"

7

Refuting Pluralism

"Christianity, if false, is of no importance,
and, if true, of infinite importance."[1]
—C.S. Lewis

 Christianity is the only true religion. Salvation
is found in Jesus Christ alone.

*"Jesus answered, 'I am the way and the truth and
the life. No one comes to the Father except through
me' "* (John 14:6).

Since the 1960s, there has been a virtual explosion of religious pluralism in this country. Christianity is no longer a consensus, but just another option in a cafeteria of religious choices. Cults and religions that used to be a minority in America are seeking mainstream status and proliferating at a geometric pace. Now Christianity is viewed by many Americans as simply one of many acceptable religions. Other "acceptable" options include Islam, Hinduism, Mormonism, Christian Science, and the Jehovah's Witnesses.

It is important to stress to your child that Jesus was very exclusive in His truth claims, indicating that what He said took precedence over all others. Jesus said He is *uniquely and exclusively* man's *only* means of coming into a relationship with God: "I am the way and the truth and the life. No one comes to the Father, but through me." Jesus warned: "Watch out that no one deceives you. For many will come in my name, claiming, 'I am the Christ,' and will deceive many.... If someone says to you, 'Look, here is the Christ!' ... do not believe it" (Matthew 24:4,5,23).

Jesus' apostles also made exclusive truth claims about Him. A bold Peter proclaimed, "There is salvation in no one else; for there is no other name under heaven that has been given among men, by which we must be saved" (Acts 4:12 NASB). Paul affirmed that "there is one God, and one mediator also between God and men, the man Christ Jesus" (1 Timothy 2:5 NASB).

Sharing Time: Train Tracks to God

There was a boy who really liked to play with his train set. The train engine pulled five train cars around the track, and it was so fun to watch it go, go, go.

Every once in a while, though, the train would go off the track. All the train cars crashed and landed beside the track. That wasn't good.

Following Jesus Christ is like staying on the train track. Following Christianity is like staying on the train track. It goes in one direction, and as long as we follow Jesus Christ and Christianity our lives are on track.

There are some people who get off the track. Instead of following Jesus and Christianity, they get involved in a different religion. They worship a different god. But the Bible tells us that those other gods are fakes. They're not real. They are false gods. Only the God of Christianity is the true God. Only Jesus is the true Savior. It's important that we follow only Him.

So, in our lives we don't want to get off the track and follow a fake god, do we? No! We want to stay on the track and only follow the true God of Christianity.[2]

8

Responding to Relativism

"A half-truth is a dangerous thing, especially if you have got hold of the wrong half."[1]

—*Myron Boyd*

 Scriptural truths are true for *all* people of *all* ages.

"Sanctify them by the truth; your word is truth" (John 17:17).

Recent polls show that among those who claim to be born-again Christians, 53 percent of those surveyed deny that there is any such thing as absolute truth.[2] This is an eye-opening statement about the low spiritual condition of the Christian church today.

Apparently many of these individuals are unaware that Christianity rests on a *foundation of absolute truth* [see 1 Kings 17:24; Psalm 43:3; 119:30; John 1:17; 17:17; 2 Timothy 2:15; 1 John 3:19; 3 John 4, 8. (*You should spend some time in these verses with your children.*)]. Absolute truth refers to statements that are true for *all people.*

Sharing Time: Traffic Laws and God's Laws

When you learn to drive a car and get your driver's license, you will have to pass a test that shows you know all the traffic laws and rules. Some of them are laws such as: "stop for red lights," "turn on your headlights when driving at night," "stay on your side of the yellow line in the road," "obey the speed limit." These laws apply to all drivers, in all vehicles, all of the time!

What would happen if everybody made up their own traffic laws? Or they decided they would obey only the laws they liked? What if some drivers decided to stop only at red lights and others decided to stop only at green lights? We would have crashes, chaos, and disaster! Traffic laws are "true" for all drivers at all times, for our own protection.

God has given us truths in His Word that are true for all people at all times. They do not change.

There are some people today who don't pay attention to the Bible. They don't listen to God's truths. Instead of following God's truths, they make up their own. That's not very smart, is it? That's like driving on the road with no traffic laws. Very dangerous!

Watch Out for Values Clarification

New Age moral relativism has entered the public schools through what is known as values clarification. Viewing human beings as intrinsically good, values clarification is a New Age ethical system that denies the moral absolutes of the Word of God. Each student is encouraged to come up with his or her own moral values. Such values are considered to be neutral (ultimately neither good nor bad). Values are determined on a strictly subjective basis.

As a result of the onslaught of moral relativism in America, Christian thinker Carl F. Henry commented that the west has lost its moral compass. There's no way to tell which way is north and which way is south when it comes to right and wrong.

As Christians, we are called to point out to the world (and fervently teach our children) that absolute morals are grounded in the absolutely moral God of the Bible. Scripture tells us: "Be perfect, therefore, as your heavenly Father is perfect" (Matthew 5:48). Moral law flows from the moral Lawgiver of the universe—God. And God stands against the moral relativist whose behavior is based on "whatever is right in his own eyes" (Deuteronomy 12:8; Proverbs 21:2).

Steps You Can Take

Because our children are surrounded by influences alien to their very beings, such as values clarification, we as parents have a sobering responsibility to guard their welfare and to lead them in the ways of the Lord. There are five key steps you as a parent can take to help insulate your child against New Age influences.[3]

1. Become educated about the various New Age influences in the public school system. There are some good books you can read on this subject (see Recommended Resources and the Bibliography).

2. Keep abreast of what your child is learning in school. Talk with your child about what he or she is learning. Be sure to scan through his or her textbooks and watch for any religious or anti-Christian elements. It is also good to volunteer in your child's classroom as often as you can. By doing this, not only will you be helpful to the school, you will also be able to observe what your child's learning environment is like.

3. Learn about and exercise your rights as a parent. For example, you can become familiar with *The Protection of Pupil Rights (Hatch) Amendment*, which says that public school instructional materials can be inspected by parents. Also become familiar with *The "Equal Protection" Clause of the Fourteenth Amendment*, which affirms that New Age educators have no more right to promote their New Age beliefs in school than do Christians to promote their beliefs.

4. Mobilize your efforts with other Christian families. Remember, a rope of many strands cannot be easily broken. By uniting with other Christians who hold the same convictions you do, your voice becomes greatly amplified. There is strength in numbers!

5. Equip your child to recognize spiritual deception. Go over important New Age buzzwords like "values clarification." Warn your child of the danger of such practices and ideas. Be sure your child knows what the Bible has to say about God, Jesus Christ, man, and salvation.

9

Debunking Humanism

> "I have come to the conclusion that the Bible is a supernatural book, that it has come from God, and that the only safety for the human race is to follow its teachings."[1]
>
> —*Salmon Chase*

Humanists will try to tell you the Bible is full of myths. Don't believe it.

"See to it that no one takes you captive through hollow and deceptive philosophy, which depends on human tradition and the basic principles of this world rather than on Christ" (Colossians 2:8).

Humanists will try to teach your children there is no supernatural, no God, no divine purpose for humanity, and no afterlife. We need to prepare our children (primarily in later childhood because of the difficulty of the subject matter) to deal with secular reasoning, theories, and arguments that conflict with genuine biblical teachings.

Elevating science to supreme authority, humanists conclude that the Bible is a fallible human document. They dismiss its miracles as the fantasies of ignorant people in biblical times who did not understand the laws of nature. They also view humanity as fundamentally good, with no sin problem.

Miracles and the Laws of Nature

Teach your children how to debunk the humanist's charge that miracles are merely the fantasies of ignorant people. People in biblical times *did* know enough of the laws of nature to recognize bona fide miracles. In fact, the reason people were so astonished at Christ's miracles was that *they did* understand the laws of nature. They knew that according to the laws of science, plain water does not normally turn into wine; dead people do not normally rise up on command; blind eyes don't normally see; deaf ears don't normally hear; and crippled people don't normally walk. When they saw Christ cause these things to happen, they knew they were witnessing something extraordinary.

Sharing Time: Walking on Water

When you go swimming, can you walk on top of the water? No, of course not.

When your mom goes swimming, can she walk on top of the water? No way!

When your dad goes swimming, can he walk on top of the water? No, of course not.

According to the laws of science, when people get into the water they normally sink unless they start swimming. Do you think people in biblical times knew that people don't normally walk on water? Of course they did.

But Jesus walked on the water! And the disciples were scared because they knew people can't walk on water (see Matthew 14:25,26). They would not have been frightened unless they had known that according to the normal laws of science human beings do not normally walk on water. Jesus really did do incredible miracles!

Science Does Not Disprove the Bible

The humanist will argue that science refutes biblical miracles. Teach your child the folly of this claim.

Science depends upon *observation* and *replication*. Without these two critical components, true science simply cannot exist. You must be able to observe the object of study and you must be able to replicate (repeat) what happened. Miracles—such as the resurrection—are by their very nature unprecedented events. No one can replicate these events in a laboratory. Hence, science cannot be the judge and jury as to whether or not these events occurred. The scientific method is useful for studying nature but not super-nature. R.C. Sproul rightly observes,

> Today when somebody steps outside of his area of expertise, people tend to follow and believe him. That is the basis of much advertising. For example, a baseball star may appear on television and promote a particular brand of razors. If that star were to tell me how to hit a baseball, he would be speaking with authority. But when he tells me the best razor blade to buy is a certain brand, then he is speaking outside of his area of expertise.

Scientists do the same type of thing in regard to miracles. They are speaking outside their field of expertise.

Certainly there is powerful evidence in support of the biblical miracles. One highly pertinent factor is the brief time that elapsed between Jesus' miraculous public ministry and the publication of the gospels. The time span was insufficient for the development of "miracle legends." Many eyewitnesses to Jesus' miracles would have still been alive to refute any untrue miracle accounts (see 1 Corinthians 15:6).

One must also recognize the noble character of the men (for example, Peter, James, and John) who witnessed these miracles. Such men were not prone to misrepresentation, and they were willing to give up their lives rather than deny their beliefs.

Sharing Time: The Truth-Tellers

Do you think that men in Bible times—such as Peter, James, and John—were lying about Jesus when they said He performed miracles? No, of course not.

The Bible says these men were honest truth-tellers. From childhood, they had been taught the Ten Commandments. One of the commandments says *do not lie* (Exodus 20:16).

These men couldn't deny the truth of Christianity, because they knew it *was* true. Did you know that some of these men were given a choice by the Roman government to either deny the truth of Christianity or be put to death? That's horrible, isn't it. But Jesus' followers knew that Jesus was real and that He really was the Savior. So they chose to give up their lives instead.

A person wouldn't give up his life for something that was a lie, would he? No—that would be stupid. But the fact that the disciples gave up their lives defending the truth of Christianity shows how strongly they believed it to be true.

Don't ever let anyone tell you that the disciples made up the story about Jesus. *They were telling the truth.*

Hostile Witnesses

There were also hostile witnesses to the miracles of Christ. When Jesus raised Lazarus from the dead, for example, none of the chief priests or Pharisees disputed the miracle (John 11:45-48). (If they could have disputed it, they would have!) The humanist needs to be reminded that because there were so many people who observed and scrutinized Christ to catch Him in error, successful fabrication of miracle stories in His ministry would have been impossible.

10

Confronting Evolution

"The evolutionists seem to know everything about the missing link except the
fact that it is missing."[1]

—*G.K. Chesterton*

 Man was directly created by the hand of God.

*"In the beginning God created the heavens and the
earth"* (Genesis 1:1).

As Christian parents, we need to make sure our children
understand that they did not evolve from apes but that they
were created by God. The following are some facts every
child should be taught regarding the creation of the universe.
(Some of these facts are too complex for young children. But
as your children mature, you will want to teach them these
things.)

1. Scientists by and large concur that *the universe had a beginning.* They may disagree as to how that beginning
   happened, but they generally agree there was a beginning. Now, the fact that there was a beginning implies
   the existence of a Beginner—a Creator. As Scripture says,
   "Every house is built by someone, but God is the builder
   of everything" (Hebrews 3:4).

2. By looking at the world and the universe around us, it
   becomes apparent that a Designer was involved. Everything is just perfect for life on earth—*so perfect* that it

gives every evidence of being designed by an intelligent God. The earth's size, composition, distance from the sun, rotational period, and many other factors are all perfect for life. The chances of there being even one planet where all of these factors *converge by accident* are almost nonexistent.[2]

3. In keeping with the above, the genetic code of all biological life on earth gives evidence of intelligent design. In fact, the information contained in genetic code is comparable to the information stored in complex computer programs. The complex design implies the existence of a Designer (God).

4. As one examines fossil records, one not only finds no evidence supporting evolution, but finds evidence against it. If evolution were true, one would expect to see in the fossil records progressively complex evolutionary forms, indicating transitions that took place. But there is no such evidence.

5. False claims are often made by evolutionists. Some people have claimed that there is scientific evidence that evolution is true. These individuals generally appeal to the fact that mutations *within* species is a proven scientific fact (microevolution). But it requires an incredible leap of logic to say that mutations *within* species proves mutations or transformations into *entirely new* species (macroevolution). You can't breed two dogs and get a cat!

Sharing Time: Man—The Image of God

Greg came home from school one day and said to his mom, "Today our teacher said that human beings evolved from apes. She believes in evolution. What do you think about evolution, Mom?"

"Well, let's answer that question by playing a silly game," Greg's mom replied. "Have you ever seen a cat give birth to a dog?"

"No way!" Greg said.

"Have you ever seen a goldfish give birth to a shark?"

"Never!"

"Have you ever heard of a lion giving birth to a monkey?"

"Impossible!" Greg said.

"Have you ever seen an orange growing on an apple tree?"

"I can't say that I have," Greg said.

"The point is," his mom said, "that everything reproduces after its kind. That's what the Bible says in the book of Genesis. That's the way God planned it. Cats give birth to cats. Goldfish give birth to goldfish. Lions give birth to lions. And apples grow on apple trees. *Everything* reproduces after its kind!"

"Now, here's something else to think about," his mom said. "The Bible says there's something true of human beings that is not true of any animal. God created human beings in His own image. And after God created man in His image, He appointed man to rule over all the animals. Obviously, then, man didn't evolve from apes but is rather over the apes and all other animals. Man is the highest part of God's creation."

Today's Dangers

1

Balancing Your Perspective on Money

"If you make money your god, it will plague you like the Devil."[1]
—*Henry Fielding*

The possession of money is not evil, but *loving* money is a root of all kinds of evil.

"For the love of money is a root of all kinds of evil. Some people, eager for money, have wandered from the faith and pierced themselves with many griefs" (1 Timothy 6:10).

"Keep your lives free from the love of money and be content with what you have, because God has said, 'Never will I leave you; never will I forsake you' " (Hebrews 13:5).

God does not condemn having possessions or riches. It is not a sin to be wealthy! (Some very godly people in the Bible—Abraham and Job, for example—were quite wealthy.) But God does condemn a *love* of possessions or riches (Luke 16:13). A love of material things is a sure sign that a person is living according to a temporal perspective and not an eternal perspective.

Help your children understand the scriptural teaching from 1 Timothy 6:9: "People who want to get rich fall into temptation and a trap and into many foolish and harmful desires that plunge men into ruin and destruction."

Jesus understandably warned His followers: "Watch out! Be on your guard against all kinds of greed; a man's life does not consist in the abundance of his possessions" (Luke 12:15). He then urged His followers to have an eternal perspective: "Do not store up for yourselves treasures on earth, where moth and rust destroy, and where thieves break in and steal. But store up for yourselves treasures in heaven" (Matthew 6:19,20; cf. John 6:27).

Sharing Time: Building Up Treasures

For this illustration you need a bottle of liquid bubbles and a blower ring.

Watch as I blow some bubbles.

What do you see? What do the bubbles do?

They look really nice for a few seconds, but then they disappear. They don't last very long. They're here one second and gone the next.

A lot of things in this world don't last. Can you count how many toys you've owned that are now broken? They seem to last for a while, but then they wear out. Nothing is lasting.

Because the things of this earth, including money, do not last, we shouldn't spend all our lives trying to get rich or to collect more things. Things will not last. And we can't take any of them with us when we die. It all stays behind.

We should set our minds not on this world but on heaven. We should build up treasures not on this world but in heaven. We can do this by obeying the things God tells us to do in the Bible.[2]

Handling Money

Our attitude should be that whether we are rich or poor (or somewhere in between), we are *stewards* of what God has provided for us. Our attitude should mirror that of the apostle Paul, who said,

> I have learned the secret of being content in any and every situation, whether well fed or hungry, whether living in plenty or in want. I can do everything through him who gives me strength (Philippians 4:12,13).

There are two disciplines you can teach your children that are a starting point for having a proper perspective on money.

1. *Tithing.* Encourage your children to give money to support the church—or perhaps a special missionary project at church (Malachi 3:10). A good round figure for tithing is 10 percent. But be careful not to communicate legalism here. There will be times in the future when your kids will want to give more than 10 percent and other times when they'll give less. This is just a ballpark figure.

   Also encourage them to give cheerfully. If their attitude is, "Rats! Ten percent down the drain!" they might as well not tithe. God loves a cheerful giver (2 Corinthians 9:7).

2. *Saving.* Whenever your kids receive an allowance or some money earned, encourage them to save some of it. Again, 10 percent is a good starting point.

In a magazine article, Susan Yates suggests giving your kids three envelopes: one for *tithing*, one for *saving*, and one for *spending*.[3] I think this is a great idea. This way your kids can easily keep track of their money.

2

A Realistic Approach to Drinking and Drugs

"Drunkenness is the ruin of a person."[1]
—*Saint Basil*

 God prohibits drunkenness, as well as ingesting any dangerous substance that can harm the body.

"Do not get drunk on wine, which leads to debauchery. Instead, be filled with the Spirit" (Ephesians 5:18).

Joe White, author of *FaithTraining*, gives us some sobering statistics on drinking in this country:

- Alcohol costs us yearly: 97,500 lives lost because of alcohol-related diseases, accidents, murders, and suicides; $100 billion-plus in economic losses; family problems in 1 out of every 4 U.S. homes.

- American children see an estimated 90,000 incidents of drinking in TV programs by the age of 21.

- Three out of ten adolescents have a drinking problem— nearly 5 million.[2]

Drinking has clearly become a grave problem in our society, and Scripture's instructions about drinking have never been more relevant. As Christian parents, we must *start early* in teaching our children what Scripture has to say about this subject.

Scripture Prohibits Drunkenness

Perhaps the place to begin is to recognize that throughout Scripture drunkenness is forbidden by God. It is not an option for the Christian. In Ephesians 5:18, the apostle Paul instructs, "Do not get drunk on wine, which leads to debauchery. Instead, be filled with the Spirit." Paul is telling us to be controlled by the Spirit, not by wine.

What Is Biblical Wine?

While drinking wine *in moderation* is permissible in Scripture (see John 2:9; 1 Timothy 3:3,8), many wine-drinking Christians today wrongly assume that what the New Testament meant by wine is identical to wine used today. This, however, is not correct. Consider the words of scholar Norman Geisler:

> Today's wine is by biblical definitions "strong drink" and hence is forbidden in the Bible! What the New Testament meant by wine was basically purified water. . . . Wine in ancient times, in Homer's day, was twenty parts water and one part wine. Twenty-to-one water is only wine-flavored water. . . . Sometimes in the ancient world they would go as strong as one part water and one part wine; this was considered strong wine. Anyone who drank wine unmixed was looked upon as a Scythian, a barbarian. So anyone who would take wine unmixed, even the Greeks thought was a barbarian. That means the Greeks would look at our culture today and say, "You Americans are barbarians—drinking straight wine." One-to-one was strong, and the average ratio in the ancient world was three or four parts water to one part wine.[3]

To give you a better handle on what all this means—to consume the amount of alcohol found in two martinis, it would take 22 glasses of New Testament wine.[4] "In other words, it is possible to become intoxicated from wine mixed with three parts water, but one's drinking would probably affect the bladder long before the mind."[5]

The Permissible Versus the Beneficial

Every Christian adult must decide for him- or herself whether or not to drink. A question we must all ask ourselves is, While drinking may be *permissible*, is it *beneficial* for me to do so? The following verses speak to this issue:

- "'Everything is permissible for me'—but not everything is beneficial. 'Everything is permissible for me'—but I will not be mastered by anything" (1 Corinthians 6:12).

- "Each of you should look not only to your own interests, but also to the interests of others" (Philippians 2:4).

- "It is better not to eat meat or drink wine or to do anything else that will cause your brother to fall" (Romans 14:21).

- "So whether you eat or drink or whatever you do, do it all for the glory of God" (1 Corinthians 10:31).

Remember that whatever you decide on this issue will be a modeling influence on your children.

Sharing Time: Taking Care of God's Home

JoAnne E. De Jonge tells a great story that illustrates the importance of taking care of our bodies, and not harming them by drinking.

We like to have a neat, clean church. After all, whom do we worship in this church? *(Pause for response.)* That's right, we worship God here. Sometimes we even call this church "God's house." Out of respect for God, because we love Him and want to honor Him, we keep our church neat and clean. We keep God's house neat and clean.

But God doesn't really live here, does He? We worship Him here, but He goes with us when we leave this church.

God doesn't live in this church because He has a far better home. God lives *in you!* . . . Did you know that God's Spirit lives in you?

The Bible says that you are God's temple—that's like His church—and that the Spirit of God lives in you.

Look at yourself: your arms, your legs, your body. God is living in that body.

Now, if we keep our church neat and clean because we worship God here, how should we keep our bodies, God's temples? (*Pause for response.*) That's right, we should keep our bodies neat and clean. We should take good care of our bodies and treat them with respect, because God's Spirit lives in us.[6]

Saying No to Drugs

Joe White tells us that some 60 billion dollars a year is spent on cocaine in the United States. More than 1,000 babies a day are born drug-damaged, and more than 100,000 a year are "crack babies."[7] And more and more teens are caught in drug addiction. Drug use has serious consequences:

- *Physically:* cocaine causes serious cardiac problems, lung dysfunction, a variety of respiratory symptoms, and is responsible for thousands of deaths.

- *Spiritually:* ingesting cocaine violates God's injunction to treat our bodies as a temple of the Holy Spirit (1 Corinthians 3:16; 6:19). We *profane* our bodies by drug abuse.

Moreover, in view of Scripture's clear command not to allow ourselves to be controlled by substances we ingest but rather be controlled by the Holy Spirit (Ephesians 5:18), the use of cocaine or other drugs is absolutely off-limits for the Christian.

Sharing Time: Blueprint for Saying No

One evening Philip was having a talk with his dad about the growing drinking and drug problems at his school. "It seems like more and more kids are trying stuff, Dad. I know it's only a matter of time before someone approaches me about joining in. It's scary!"

"Philip," his dad said, "have you thought out what you're going to say if that moment does come? Do you have a plan?"

Philip answered, "I don't know. I mean, I'm not going to drink or take drugs or anything. That's for sure. But I haven't really thought about what I'll say."

His dad said, "Son, when a foreman is working with builders at a building site, does he just tell them, 'Okay, here are some nails and wood. Go start hammering things together. Hopefully you'll build a nice building.'"

"No," Philip replied, "they build according to a plan—a blueprint, right?"

"That's right," Philip's dad said. "Something like that is just too important to go into without a plan."

Philip's dad continued, "When a surgeon is going to do open-heart surgery on a patient, does he begin cutting wherever he feels like cutting, without a well-thought-out plan and procedure?"

"No way!" Philip said. "The patient would probably die, right?"

"That's right," Philip's dad said. "The surgeon operates according to medically accepted plans and procedures. Obviously, something like open-heart surgery is too important to go into without a plan. It's a life and death matter.

"In the same way," his dad continued, "saying no to drugs and drinking can ultimately be a life-and-death matter. It is too important a matter to face without a plan. It's important for you to think out *in advance* what to say when someone invites you to drink or take drugs."

"Boy, that sounds like good advice, Dad," Philip said.

That night Philip gave serious thought to exactly what he would say if he were invited to drink or take drugs. He even rehearsed his words aloud!

3

Your Kids and Sex

"Satan fails to speak of the remorse, the futility, the loneliness, and the spiritual devastation which go hand in hand with immorality."[1]

—*Billy Graham*

 God calls us to flee from all forms of sexual immorality.

"The body is not meant for sexual immorality, but for the Lord, and the Lord for the body" (1 Corinthians 6:13).

"Flee from sexual immorality. All other sins a man commits are outside his body, but he who sins sexually sins against his own body" (1 Corinthians 6:18).

"It is God's will that you should be sanctified: that you should avoid sexual immorality" (1 Thessalonians 4:3).

Did you know—

- A survey of 1,400 kids revealed that by age 18, 43 percent of churched youth have engaged in sexual intercourse, and another 18 percent have fondled breasts or genitals.[2]

- In the next 24 hours more than 35,000 Americans will become infected with a sexually transmitted disease. That amounts to 13 million people in the next year.[3]

- Adult bookstores in the United States outnumber McDonald's restaurants by a margin of at least three to one.[4]

- The pornography industry grosses nearly $8 billion annually.[5]

- Some 400 million adult (pornographic) tapes were rented from mainstream video outlets in 1990.[6]

Sexual immorality has become a huge, huge problem in this country. Because our children are sure to confront this problem in a big way as they mature, we must do all we can to educate them not only regarding the physical dangers of promiscuous sex but also regarding a biblical view of sex.

A Biblical View of Sex

God created human beings as sexual beings. But He intended sexual activity to be confined to the marriage relationship. Unfortunately, as is true with so many other things, many people have taken that which God intended for good and have perverted its use. The result? Sexual enslavement.

Scripture has a lot to say about human sexuality:

- Scripture is consistent in its emphasis that a sexual relationship can only be engaged in within the confines of marriage (1 Corinthians 7:2).

- The apostles urged all Christians to abstain from fornication (Acts 15:20).

- Paul said that the body is not for fornication and that a man should flee it (1 Corinthians 6:13,18).

- Adultery is condemned in Scripture (Exodus 20:14).

- In the Old Testament, adulterers were to be put to death (Leviticus 20:10).

- Jesus pronounced adultery wrong even in its basic motives (Matthew 5:27,28).

- Paul called adultery an evil work of the flesh (Galatians 5:19).

- In Revelation 21:8, John was told that for those who practiced adultery, "their place will be in the fiery lake of burning sulfur."

Sex within marriage, however, is good (see Genesis 2:24; Matthew 19:5; 1 Corinthians 6:16; Ephesians 5:31). Sex is part of God's wonderful creation. Indeed, He created sex and "everything created by God is good." But it is good *only* within the confines of the marriage relationship (see Hebrews 13:4).

God Is Not a Cosmic Killjoy

Some children may view God (with His commandments on sex) as some kind of cosmic killjoy who denies us all our fun. But this is not the case at all. Josh McDowell has some great insights here:

> One of the greatest truths you can share with your child about saying no is that inherent within every negative command in the Bible there are two positive principles: 1) it is meant to protect us, and 2) to provide for us.
>
> God knows that if sex is going to be meaningful, it must be experienced within a loving commitment of marriage. His laws, restrictions, and commands are actually for our good (Deuteronomy 10:12,13). They establish the boundaries and guidelines that define maximum love, relationships, and sex.
>
> As much as possible, explain to your children this basic truth behind the restrictions God places upon them. Be sure to communicate that both you and God want only what is best for them. Eventually the point will get through; you love them, and your loving limits—that come from a loving God—are to protect and provide for them.[7]

Sharing Time: Don't Cross the Line

Jeff came home after a day at the beach with some of his friends. As soon as he walked in the door, his dad immediately noticed that he seemed to be shaken up.

"Are you okay?" Jeff's dad asked.

"We had a close call today at the beach," Jeff said. "Steve almost drowned."

"Oh no! Is he okay?" his dad asked.

"Yes, but he came so close to drowning that it was scary," Jeff said.

Jeff then explained what happened. "Steve didn't obey the rules. There was a sign that said, 'No Swimming Beyond This Point—Dangerous Undercurrents.' I told Steve not to go beyond the sign, but he said, 'Oh, I'm not scared. I'm a strong swimmer. There's nothing to worry about.' He was okay at first, but then he just got swept away. He got in way over his head, and he was pulled under by the current. The situation was totally out of his control. Luckily a lifeguard managed to get there in time to rescue him, but it was close."

"Thank goodness he's okay. I'll bet Steve learned a good lesson!" Jeff's father said.

"I think he did, and I did too! We need to remember that the rules and limits are there for our own good." Jeff said.

"Right!" his dad said.

"And you know," his dad continued, "I think this lesson can apply to something you asked me about earlier this week regarding that party you went to last Saturday. Remember when you said some of the guys were getting into heavy kissing and who knows what else with their girlfriends that night?"

"I think I know where you're heading with this, Dad. There are certain points past which we should never 'swim' in our relationships before marriage."

"That's right," his dad replied. "Many times young people seem to think they can handle crossing the line of premarital sex. But then—like being pulled under water by a strong current—they completely lose control of the situation and end up way over their heads, ruining their lives or the lives of other people. So it's very important that we recognize that God's rules about premarital sex are for our own good. There are certain points in a relationship beyond which an unmarried person should *never* go, no matter how strong they think they are!"

4

Saying No to Suicide

"In our hearts we felt the sentence of
death. But this happened that we might
not rely on ourselves but on God."
—*2 Corinthians 1:9*

 No matter how bleak things may look, suicide
is never the answer.

"You shall not murder" (Exodus 20:13).

Did you know—

- Every 90 minutes a teenager commits suicide in this
country.

- Eighteen teens will end their lives each and every day.

- Thirty percent of teenagers who survive a suicide make
another attempt within two years.[1]

Suicide is a gigantic problem in this country. For this
reason, it is critically important not only that you be well informed about this issue but that your children develop a
Christian perspective on it.

Experts tell us that when young people enter adolescence
they experience tremendous change and stress in their lives.
The combination of peer pressure, the drive for independence,
coming into sexual awareness, the possibility of substance

abuse (drinking and drugs), and so forth, can create immeasurable confusion and frustration in a young person's mind.[2] Tragically, many teens deal with this confusion and frustration with suicide.

The experts also tell us that we should *never* ignore a threat to commit suicide. "If someone talks about ending his life, listen. People who talk about suicide are serious."[3] If you think your child is threatening suicide to get attention, give him attention. He or she needs serious help.

It is a fact that 8 of every 10 people who commit suicide give some indication of their intention in something they say or do.[4] For this reason, it is important that parents be aware of suicidal warning signs to watch for. Dr. Michael P. Mastroianni provides this list:

- Sudden change in eating or sleeping patterns.

- Preoccupation with death and the expression of suicidal thoughts.

- A definite plan for committing the act.

- Making final arrangements like giving away prized possessions or writing a will.

- Withdrawing from friends and family.

- Dramatic changes in school—failing grades, quitting activities, skipping classes.

- Alcohol or drug use.

- Changes in personality like aggressiveness, nervousness, or apathy.

- Depression over the loss of a boyfriend or girlfriend.[5]

If you witness some of these symptoms in your child, be on the alert. Take action. Get intimately involved in the life of your child. And get professional help now!

What Does the Bible Say About Suicide?

Beyond understanding the above factors, it is critically important for both parents and their children to understand what Scripture has to say about the issue of suicide.

From a biblical perspective, issues of life and death lie in the sovereign hands of God alone. Job said to God, "Man's days are determined; you [God] have decreed the number of his months and have set limits he cannot exceed" (Job 14:5). David said to God, "All the days ordained for me were written in your book before one of them came to be" (Psalm 139:16).

Moreover, suicide goes against the commandments of God. In fact, the sixth commandment tells us, "You shall not murder" (Exodus 20:13). This command is based on the sanctity of human life. We must remember that man was created in the image of God (Genesis 1:26).

It is important to understand that the command "you shall not murder," has no direct object. It doesn't say, "You shall not murder *someone else*," or "You shall not murder *your fellow man*." It simply says, "You shall not murder." The prohibition thus includes not just the murder of one's fellow man but even the murder of oneself.[6] While suicide is certainly not the "unforgivable sin,"[7] we must never forget that God prohibits murder of *any* kind.

Christian pastors and counselors often point out that a believer who ends his life also forever ends his opportunities to witness and serve the Lord on earth. Furthermore, suicide is one of the greatest acts of selfishness, for in it the individual caters to his own desires and his own will, ignoring the catastrophic effects it has on others.

The lives of certain biblical saints are instructive on the issue of suicide. There were times when certain servants of God were so severely tested and distressed that they wished for their own death (see 1 Kings 19:4; Jonah 4:8). But these individuals did not take matters into their own hands and kill themselves. Instead, in these cases, *God always rescued them.* We can learn a lesson here. When we despair, we must turn to God and not commit suicide. *God will see us through.*

The apostle Paul certainly went through tough times. Indeed, in 2 Corinthians 1:8, Paul reflected on his past: "We do not want you to be uninformed, brothers, about the hardships we suffered in the province of Asia. We were under great pressure, far beyond our ability to endure, so that *we despaired even of life*" (emphasis added). Nevertheless, Paul did not succumb to breaking God's commandment against murder by committing suicide. He depended on God, and God came through. God gave Paul all the sustenance he needed to make it through his ordeal.

Following Paul's example, *we* must depend on God when life looks bleak and hopeless. And just as God sustained Paul through his difficulties, so He will sustain us.

Sharing Time: You Are Never Alone!

Charlotte came to her mother one day and said, "Mom, our teacher told us that a girl in our school committed suicide last night. I don't know her personally, but isn't that terrible?"

"Oh, that is terrible. What was her name?" her mom asked.

"Her name was Jane."

"Did your teacher know any details about why she committed suicide?" her mom asked.

"All we were told is that she had been very depressed about things at school and her home life."

"I'm so sorry to hear that," her mom said.

"Mom, why did she have to commit suicide?"

"She didn't have to—and that's what makes it so tragic. You know, there are a lot of people who get depressed about things at one time or another. Even people in biblical times got depressed. But suicide is never the answer. That's the worst decision a person could ever make. God wants us to depend on Him whenever things get tough. He will always come through for us.

"And honey, since this subject has come up, let me say something else. If you ever get depressed about anything—anything at all—never, ever think that you are alone. Both your mom and dad are here for you. And God is here for you, too! You never have to be alone when life seems hard. So don't try to go it alone. Let us help. Okay?"

"Okay, Mom. Thanks."

Additional Help

A Note of Encouragement

In the introduction of this book I mentioned a "Peanuts" comic strip in which there was a conversation between Lucy and Charlie Brown. Lucy had said that life was like a deck chair: Some people place it so they can see where they are going; some place it so they can see where they have been; and some place it so they can see where they are at present.

Charlie Brown replied: "I can't even get mine unfolded."

I noted that many people feel just like Charlie Brown when it comes to raising Christian children in a non-Christian world. Hopefully, though, after having read this book, you can now at least get your chair unfolded.

In this book I've compared the teaching and training of our children to passing a baton to them in a relay race. Passing the baton represents passing onto them the scriptural principles from the Bible they need in order to live a successful Christian life.

I hope that you've made (and will *continue* to make) these principles a part of your life's fabric. We should not assume that teaching our children these truths a single time will stick with them throughout life. We need to *continually* and *persistently* teach them to our children. And by the time they leave home, the principles will have become a part of *their* fabric. That's the goal.

Now, as a runner passing the baton to your child, there will inevitably come times when you manage to drop the baton and trip over your own feet. We all blow it from time to time. When that happens to you, God's desire is that you pick up the baton, stand up straight, dust yourself off, and get back in the race. Remember—God is a master at using weak vessels to accomplish His purposes. God's strength is made perfect in our weakness as we seek to faithfully fulfill our stewardship by being good parents. Trust in God. *He will help you.*

Notes

Charlie Brown Says . . .
1. Larry Christenson, *The Christian Family* (Minneapolis: Bethany Fellowship, 1974), p. 55.
2. Mayo Mathers, "What My Children Have Taught Me About God," *Today's Christian Woman*, 1994. Electronic on-line version downloaded from America Online.
3. Howard Hendricks, *Heaven Help the Home!* (Wheaton, IL: Victor Books, 1982), p. 12.

Evangelizing Your Children
1. John Gill in *The Online Bible* (electronic media), version 2.5.2.
2. *Draper's Book of Quotations for the Christian World* (Wheaton, IL: Tyndale House Publishers, 1992), p. 106.
3. Charles Spurgeon in *Spurgeon Quotes*, electronic media, Hypercard database.
4. Eric Stuyck, "Can Children Be Saved?" Child Evangelism Fellowship of Frederick County, Maryland, downloaded from America Online.
5. Ibid.

Teaching Your Children
1. Isidore Epstein, *The Jewish Way of Life* (London: N.p., 1946), cited in William Barclay, *Educational Ideals in the Ancient World* (Grand Rapids: Baker Book House, 1974), p. 15.
2. Lawrence O. Richards, *A Theology of Christian Education* (Grand Rapids: Zondervan Publishing House, 1979), p. 186.
3. Ray Stedman, "Life: The Teacher," 18 February 1973, *Guidelines for the Home* series, Peninsula Bible Church, downloaded from the Internet.
4. Ibid.

Training Your Children
1. *Draper's Book of Quotations for the Christian World* (Wheaton, IL: Tyndale House Publishers, 1992), p. 318.
2. Based on class notes from Dr. Howard Hendricks's course "The Christian Home" (#726), taught at Dallas Theological Seminary, 1980.
3. Kathi Hudson, *Raising Kids God's Way* (Wheaton, IL: Crossway Books, 1995), p. 14.
4. Ibid., p. 14.
5. Ibid., p. 92.
6. Ibid., p. 95.
7. Ibid.
8. Ray Stedman, "What Every Child Should Know," *Guidelines for the Home* series, Peninsula Bible Church, downloaded from the Internet.

Modeling for Your Children
1. Jean Fleming, *A Mother's Heart* (Colorado Springs: NavPress, 1987), p. 65.
2. *Bible Illustrations for Preaching*, electronic media, Hypercard database, ©1991 by Michael Green.
3. Kathi Hudson, *Raising Kids God's Way* (Wheaton, IL: Crossway Books, 1995), p. 43.
4. Lawrence O. Richards, *A Theology of Christian Education* (Grand Rapids: Zondervan Publishing House, 1979), pp. 84-85; see also Hudson, *Raising Kids*, p. 125.

Love and Time—Ties That Bind
1. *Draper's Book of Quotations for the Christian World* (Wheaton, IL: Tyndale House Publishers, 1992), p. 510.
2. Armand Nicholi, "What Do We Know About Successful Families?" This monograph is available from Grad Resources, 13612 Midway Road, Suite 500, Dallas, TX 75244.
3. Ibid.

4. Ross Campbell, *How to Really Love Your Child* (Wheaton, IL: Victor Books, 1977), p. 30.
5. A good place to begin is Campbell's book *How to Really Love Your Child.*
6. Campbell, *How to Really Love,* p. 59.
7. Ibid., pp. 59-60.
8. Russell Chandler, *Racing Toward 2001* (Grand Rapids: Zondervan Publishing House, 1992), p. 93.
9. Kathi Hudson, *Raising Kids God's Way* (Wheaton, IL: Crossway Books, 1995), p. 35.
10. Howard Hendricks, *Heaven Help the Home!* (Wheaton, IL: Victor Books, 1982), p. 69, emphasis added.
11. George Barna, *The Future of the American Family* (Chicago: Moody Press, 1993), p. 105.
12. Ibid.
13. *Bits & Pieces,* 24 June 1993, pp. 13-14.
14. Hendricks, *Heaven Help the Home!* p. 34.

Making the Most of Family Devotions

1. Paul Lee Tan, *Encyclopedia of 7,700 Illustrations* (Rockville, MD: Assurance Publishers, 1985), p. 1064.
2. Kathi Hudson, *Raising Kids God's Way* (Wheaton, IL: Crossway Books, 1995), p. 22.
3. Kathi Hudson has some great ideas for family devotionals. See *Raising Kids,* p. 22.
4. Credit goes to Kathi Hudson for this idea.

The Boundaries of Love—Family Rules

1. *Draper's Book of Quotations for the Christian World* (Wheaton, IL: Tyndale House Publishers, 1992), p. 458.
2. *Raising Them Right: Focus on the Family Offers Its Best Advice on Child-Rearing* (Colorado Springs: Focus on the Family Publishing, 1994), p. 29.
3. *Bible Illustrations for Preaching,* electronic media, Hypercard database, ©1991 by Michael Green.
4. Larry Christenson, *The Christian Family* (Minneapolis: Bethany Fellowship, 1974), p. 78.
5. Ray Stedman, "Parents and Children," *Guidelines for the Home* series, Peninsula Bible Church, downloaded from the Internet.
6. Ibid.
7. Howard Hendricks, *Heaven Help the Home!* (Wheaton, IL: Victor Books, 1982), p. 52.
8. Christenson, *Christian Family,* p. 58.
9. Hendricks, *Heaven Help the Home!* p. 56.

Teaching Responsibility

1. *Draper's Book of Quotations for the Christian World* (Wheaton, IL: Tyndale House Publishers, 1992), p. 212.

Walking in Humility

1. *Draper's Book of Quotations for the Christian World* (Wheaton, IL: Tyndale House Publishers, 1992), p. 325.
2. *Bible Illustrations for Preaching,* electronic media, Hypercard database, ©1991 by Michael Green.

A Willingness to Learn

1. *Draper's Book of Quotations for the Christian World* (Wheaton, IL: Tyndale House Publishers, 1992), p. 506.
2. Paul Lee Tan, *Encyclopedia of 7,700 Illustrations* (Rockville, MD: Assurance Publishers, 1985), p. 370.
3. *Bible Illustrations for Preaching,* electronic media, Hypercard database, ©1991 by Michael Green.

An Honest Heart

1. *Draper's Book of Quotations for the Christian World* (Wheaton, IL: Tyndale House Publishers, 1992), p. 318.

2. *Bible Illustrations for Preaching*, electronic media, Hypercard database, ©1991 by Michael Green.

A Kind Heart
1. *Draper's Book of Quotations for the Christian World* (Wheaton, IL: Tyndale House Publishers, 1992), p. 90.
2. Emily Hunter, *A Child's First Steps to Virtues* (Eugene, OR: Harvest House Publishers, 1995), p. 112.

A Generous Heart
1. *Draper's Book of Quotations for the Christian World* (Wheaton, IL: Tyndale House Publishers, 1992), p. 234.
2. Paul Lee Tan, *Encyclopedia of 7,700 Illustrations* (Rockville, MD: Assurance, 1985), p. 478.
3. *Draper's Book of Quotations*, p. 235.
4. Emily Hunter, *A Child's First Steps to Virtues* (Eugene, OR: Harvest House Publishers, 1995), p. 34.

Good Work Habits
1. *Draper's Book of Quotations for the Christian World* (Wheaton, IL: Tyndale House Publishers, 1992), p. 373.
2. I am indebted to Jean Lush for these helpful suggestions. See "Teaching Children to Work," in *Raising Them Right* (Colorado Springs: Focus on the Family Publishing, 1994), pp. 66-70.

Success God's Way
1. *Draper's Book of Quotations for the Christian World* (Wheaton, IL: Tyndale House Publishers, 1992), p. 591.
2. Paul Lee Tan, *Encyclopedia of 7,700 Illustrations* (Rockville, MD: Assurance, 1985), p. 1373.
3. Kathi Hudson, *Raising Kids God's Way* (Wheaton, IL: Crossway Books, 1995), p. 64.

Controlling Emotions
1. *Draper's Book of Quotations for the Christian World* (Wheaton, IL: Tyndale House Publishers, 1992), p. 170.
2. *Bible Illustrations for Preaching*, electronic media, Hypercard database, ©1991 by Michael Green.
3. Sheryl Bruinsma, *Object Lessons Using Children's Toys* (Grand Rapids: Baker Book House, 1996), p. 62. Used by permission.
4. Ross Campbell, "Quench the Embers of Anger," *Single-Parent Family*, ©1996, downloaded from "Focus on the Family" site on America Online.

Handling Failure
1. Paul Lee Tan, *Encyclopedia of 7,700 Illustrations* (Rockville, MD: Assurance, 1985), p. 1373.
2. *Draper's Book of Quotations for the Christian World* (Wheaton, IL: Tyndale House Publishers, 1992), p. 197.
3. Howard Hendricks, *Heaven Help the Home!* (Wheaton, IL: Victor Books, 1982), p. 61.
4. Kathi Hudson, *Raising Kids God's Way* (Wheaton, IL: Crossway Books, 1995), p. 197.
5. Adapted from Joe White, *Faith Training* (Colorado Springs: Focus on the Family Publishing, 1994), p. 226.
6. *Draper's Book of Quotations*, p. 196

Making Wise Decisions
1. *Draper's Book of Quotations for the Christian World* (Wheaton, IL: Tyndale House Publishers, 1992), p. 614.
2. Les Parrott, "Grades and Grace," in *Raising Them Right* (Colorado Springs: Focus on the Family Publishing, 1994), p. 237.

3. Kathi Hudson, *Raising Kids God's Way* (Wheaton, IL: Crossway Books, 1995), p. 147.
4. Sheryl Bruinsma, *Object Lessons Using Children's Toys* (Grand Rapids: Baker Book House, 1996), p. 82. Used by permission.
5. Susan Yates, "Helping Your Child Make Choices," *Today's Christian Woman*, 1994, downloaded from "Christianity Today" site on America Online.
6. Adapted from *In-the-Bag Stories: Object Talks for Children*, 1990, p. 35. By Louise Kohr. Used by permission of Standard Publishing Company, Cincinnati, OH.

Speaking in a God-Honoring Way
1. *Draper's Book of Quotations for the Christian World* (Wheaton, IL: Tyndale House Publishers, 1992), p. 622.
2. Adapted from *26 More Object Talks for Children's Worship*, 1990, pp. 38-39. By Virginia Ann Van Seters. Used by permission of Standard Publishing Company, Cincinnati, OH.
3. Card deck of illustrations, Dallas Theological Seminary, 3909 Swiss Avenue, Dallas, TX 75204.
4. Adapted from JoAnne E. De Jonge, *All-Occasion Object Lessons* (Grand Rapids: Baker Book House, 1996), p. 108. Used by permission.

Gaining a Healthy Self-Concept
1. *Draper's Book of Quotations for the Christian World* (Wheaton, IL: Tyndale House Publishers, 1992), p. 549.
2. Susan Yates, "Boosting Your Child's Body Image," *Today's Christian Woman*, 1995; downloaded from "Christianity Today" site on America Online.
3. Ibid.
4. Adapted from JoAnne E. De Jonge, *More Object Lessons from Nature* (Grand Rapids: Baker Book House, 1991), p. 73. Used by permission.

Dealing with Peers
1. *Bible Illustrations*, electronic media (Hypercard stack for Macintosh).
2. Norman Bull; cited in Lawrence Richards, *A Theology of Christian Education* (Grand Rapids: Zondervan Publishing House, 1979), p. 82.
3. These tips are based on Susan Yates, "When You Don't Like Your Kid's Friends," *Today's Christian Woman*, 1996; downloaded from the "Christianity Today" site on America Online.

God's Book—The Bible
1. Draper's Book of Quotations for the Christian World (Wheaton, IL: Tyndale House Publishers, 1992), p. 36.
2. Adapted from *Object Talks for Preschoolers*, 1996, p. 43. By Sandra Crosser. Used by permission of Standard Publishing Company, Cincinnati, OH.
3. J.I. Packer, *Knowing Christianity* (Wheaton, IL: Harold Shaw Publishers, 1995), p. 16.
4. Adapted from *Easy Object Talks for Teaching Children*, 1992, p. 22. By Virginia Ann Van Seters. Used by permission of Standard Publishing Company, Cincinnati, OH.
5. See Ron Rhodes, *The Culting of America* (Eugene, OR: Harvest House Publishers, 1994), p. 42.
6. Susan Yates, "Are Your Kids Hungry for God's Word?" *Today's Christian Woman*, 1995, downloaded from "Christianity Today" site on America Online.
7. Ibid.
8. Adapted from JoAnne E. De Jonge, *More Object Lessons from Nature* (Grand Rapids: Baker Book House, 1991), p. 10. Used by permission.
9. *Raising Them Right* (Colorado Springs: Focus on the Family Publishing, 1994), pp. 72-75.
10. Adapted from De Jonge, *More Object Lessons*, p. 36. Used by permission.

Getting to Know God
1. Psalm 68:35.

2. Adapted from JoAnne E. De Jonge, *All-Occasion Object Lessons* (Grand Rapids: Baker Book House, 1996), p. 75. Used by permission.

God and Man
1. Adapted from *Object Talks for Preschoolers*, 1996, p. 7. By Sandra Crosser. Used by permission of Standard Publishing Company, Cincinnati, OH. See also Robert S. Coombs, *Enlightening Object Lessons for Children* (Grand Rapids: Baker Book House, 1994), p. 36. Used by permission.
2. Ibid, p. 21. Used by permission.
3. Ibid., p. 34. Used by permission.
4. Adapted from *Easy Object Talks for Teaching Children*, 1992, p. 14. By Virginia Ann Van Seters. Used by permission of Standard Publishing Company, Cincinnati, OH.
5. Adapted from Ibid., p. 10. Used by permission.

The True Jesus
1. *Draper's Book of Quotations for the Christian World* (Wheaton, IL: Tyndale House Publishers, 1992), p. 66.
2. J. Allan Peterson, *Leadership*, 5:2, electronic on-line version downloaded from America Online.
3. Adapted from JoAnne E. De Jonge, *More Object Lessons from Nature* (Grand Rapids: Baker Book House, 1991), p. 133. Used by permission.
4. Adapted from JoAnne E. De Jonge, *All-Occasion Object Lessons* (Grand Rapids: Baker Book House, 1996), p. 158. Used by permission.

All About Sin and Salvation
1. *Draper's Book of Quotations for the Christian World* (Wheaton, IL: Tyndale House Publishers, 1992), p. 539.
2. Adapted from JoAnne E. De Jonge, *All-Occasion Object Lessons* (Grand Rapids: Baker Book House, 1996), p. 121. Used by permission.
3. Adapted from *Object Talks for Preschoolers*, 1996, p. 32. By Sandra Crosser. Used by permission of Standard Publishing Company, Cincinnati, OH.
4. Adapted from Ibid., p. 32. Used by permission.

The Family of God—The Church
1. *Draper's Book of Quotations for the Christian World* (Wheaton, IL: Tyndale House Publishers, 1992), p. 79.
2. Charles Swindoll, *Growing Deep in the Christian Life* (Portland, OR: Multnomah, 1986), p. 339.
3. John Wesley, cited in Blanchard, *More Gathered Gold* (Hertfordshire, England: Evangelical Press, 1986), p. 43.
4. *Draper's Book of Quotations*, p. 83.
5. In John Blanchard, *More Gathered Gold*, p. 38.
6. Adapted from Robert S. Coombs, *Enlightening Object Lessons for Children* (Grand Rapids: Baker Book House, 1994), p. 69. Used by permission.
7. Sheryl Bruinsma, *Object Lessons Using Children's Toys* (Grand Rapids: Baker Book House, 1996), p. 8. Used by permission.
8. Russell Chandler, *Racing Toward 2001* (Grand Rapids: Zondervan Publishing House, 1992), p. 112.
9. Adapted from *26 More Object Talks for Children's Worship*, 1990, p. 12. By Virginia Ann Van Seters. Used by permission of Standard Publishing Company, Cincinnati, OH.

Power from on High—The Holy Spirit
1. *Draper's Book of Quotations for the Christian World* (Wheaton, IL: Tyndale House Publishers, 1992), p. 315.
2. Paul Lee Tan, *Encyclopedia of 7,700 Illustrations* (Rockville, MD: Assurance, 1985), p. 555.

Winning Battles—The World, the Sin Nature, and the Devil
1. Adapted from JoAnne E. De Jonge, *More Object Lessons from Nature* (Grand Rapids: Baker Book House, 1991), p. 68. Used by permission.
2. Adapted from Ibid., p. 140. Used by permission.

Angels Among Us
1. *Draper's Book of Quotations for the Christian World* (Wheaton, IL: Tyndale House Publishers, 1992), p. 19.
2. Ron Rhodes, *Angels Among Us* (Eugene, OR: Harvest House Publishers, 1995), p. 20.
3. Billy Graham, *Angels: God's Secret Agents* (Garden City, NY: Doubleday & Co., 1975), p. 152.

Spiritual Growth
1. *Draper's Book of Quotations for the Christian World* (Wheaton, IL: Tyndale House Publishers, 1992), p. 585.
2. John Maxwell, "Getting to Know God with Your Children," Focus on the Family, 1995, downloaded from "Focus on the Family" site on America Online.
3. Eric Stuyck, "Can God Use Children?" *Vision*, monthly newsletter of Child Evangelism Fellowship, downloaded from America Online.
4. Adapted from *Easy Object Talks for Teaching Children*, 1992, p. 6. By Virginia Ann Van Seters. Used by permission of Standard Publishing Company, Cincinnati, OH.
5. Joe White, *FaithTraining* (Colorado Springs: Focus on the Family Publishing, 1994), p. 74.
6. Rick Warren, *The Purpose-Driven Church* (Grand Rapids: Zondervan Publishing House, 1996), p. 370.

Cult-Proofing Your Kids
1. Cited in Russell Chandler, "The Changing Church," *Moody Monthly*, January 1992, p. 13.
2. J. Isamu Yamamoto, "The Buddha," *Christian Research Journal*, Spring/Summer 1994, p. 10.

Refuting Reincarnation
1. Shirley MacLaine, *Out on a Limb* (New York: Bantam Books, 1983), p. 233.

Unmasking Eastern Meditation
1. *Draper's Book of Quotations for the Christian World* (Wheaton, IL: Tyndale House Publishers, 1992), p. 422.

Panning Pantheism
1. A.W. Tozer, *The Knowledge of the Holy* (New York: Harper & Row, 1961), p. 75.

Avoiding Astrology
1. Phillip Schaff, *History of the Christian Church* (Grand Rapids: Eerdmans, 1960), vol. 6, p. 470.

Refusing Religious Pluralism
1. *Draper's Book of Quotations for the Christian World* (Wheaton, IL: Tyndale House Publishers, 1992), p. 66.
2. Adapted from Robert S. Coombs, *Enlightening Object Lessons for Children* (Grand Rapids: Baker Book House, 1994), p. 18.

Responding to Relativism
1. *Draper's Book of Quotations for the Christian World* (Wheaton, IL: Tyndale House Publishers, 1992), p. 626.
2. George Barna, *What Americans Believe* (Ventura, CA: Regal Books, 1991), p. 36.
3. Adapted from Berit Kjos, *Your Child and the New Age* (Wheaton, IL: Victor Books, 1990), pp. 28-37.

Debunking Humanism

1. *Draper's Book of Quotations for the Christian World* (Wheaton, IL: Tyndale House Publishers, 1992), p. 42.

Confronting Evolution

1. *Draper's Book of Quotations for the Christian World* (Wheaton, IL: Tyndale House Publishers, 1992), p. 111.
2. CRI Perspective, "Creation versus Evolution," © Christian Research Institute, Irvine, California.

Balancing Your Perspective on Money

1. *Draper's Book of Quotations for the Christian World* (Wheaton, IL: Tyndale House Publishers, 1992), p. 426.
2. Adapted from JoAnne E. De Jonge, *More Object Lessons from Nature* (Grand Rapids: Baker Book House, 1991), p. 59. Used by permission.
3. Susan Yates, "Dollars and Sense," *Today's Christian Woman*, 1996, downloaded from the "Christianity Today" site on America Online.

A Realistic Approach to Drinking and Drugs

1. *Draper's Book of Quotations for the Christian World* (Wheaton, IL: Tyndale House Publishers, 1992), p. 17.
2. Joe White, *FaithTraining* (Colorado Springs: Focus on the Family Publishing, 1994), pp. 287-88.
3. Norman Geisler, "Wine, Whiskey, and the Word of God," 1981. Unpublished handout at Dallas Theological Seminary.
4. Ibid.
5. Ibid.
6. Adapted from JoAnne E. De Jonge, *More Object Lessons from Nature* (Grand Rapids: Baker Book House, 1991), p. 86. Used by permission.
7. White, *FaithTraining*, pp. 289-90.

Your Kids and Sex

1. *Draper's Book of Quotations for the Christian World* (Wheaton, IL: Tyndale House Publishers, 1992), p. 148.
2. Josh McDowell, "Reasons to Wait," in *Raising Them Right* (Colorado Springs: Focus on the Family Publishers, 1994), p. 102.
3. Ibid., p. 104.
4. Joe White, *FaithTraining* (Colorado Springs: Focus on the Family Publishing, 1994), p. 291.
5. Ibid., p. 291.
6. Ibid., p. 291.
7. McDowell, "Reasons," p. 103.

Saying No to Suicide

1. Michael P. Mastroianni, "When a Student Cries for Help," Teachers in Focus, 1995; downloaded from "Focus on the Family" site on America Online.
2. Ibid.
3. Ibid.
4. Ibid.
5. Ibid.
6. See Charles Ryrie, *You Mean the Bible Teaches That* (Chicago: Moody Press, 1978), p. 78.
7. Some sensitive Christians have wondered if committing suicide causes one to lose his or her salvation, leading to an eternity in hell. There is no scriptural justification for such a harsh view. Scripture indicates that those who have trusted in Christ are saved forever and will never lose their salvation (see Romans 8:30; Ephesians 4:30).

Recommended Resources

There are many good resources at your local Christian bookstore that provide object lessons and illustrations for teaching your children. The following are some that I recommend.

Bruinsma, Sheryl. *Object Lessons Using Children's Toys*. Grand Rapids: Baker Book House, 1996.

Coombs, Robert S. *Enlightening Object Lessons for Children*. Grand Rapids: Baker Book House, 1992.

Crosser, Sandra. *Object Talks for Preschoolers*. Cincinnati, OH: Standard Publishing, 1996.

DeJonge, JoAnne E. *All-Occasion Object Lessons*. Grand Rapids: Baker Book House, 1996.

DeJonge, JoAnne E. *More Object Lessons from Nature*. Grand Rapids: Baker Book House, 1991.

Kohr, Louise. *In-the-Bag Stories: Object Talks for Children*. Cincinnati: Standard Publishing, 1990.

Van Seters, Virginia Ann. *26 More Object Talks for Children's Worship*. Cincinnati: Standard Publishing, 1990.

Van Seters, Virginia Ann. *Easy Object Talks for Teaching Children*. Cincinnati: Standard Publishing, 1992.

Bibliography

Barclay, William. *Educational Ideals in the Ancient World*. Grand Rapids: Baker Book House, 1974.

Barna, George. *The Future of the American Family*. Chicago: Moody Press, 1993.

_____. *What Americans Believe*. Ventura, CA: Regal Books, 1991.

Blanchard, John. *More Gathered Gold*. Hertfordshire, England: Evangelical Press, 1986.

Bruinsma, Sheryl. *Object Lessons Using Children's Toys*. Grand Rapids: Baker Book House, 1996.

Campbell, Ross. *How to Really Love Your Child*. Wheaton, IL: Victor Books, 1977.

Chandler, Russell. *Racing Toward 2001*. Grand Rapids: Zondervan Publishing House, 1992.

Christenson, Larry. *The Christian Family*. Minneapolis: Bethany Fellowship, 1974.

Coombs, Robert S. *Enlightening Object Lessons for Children*. Grand Rapids: Baker Book House, 1992.

Crosser, Sandra. *Object Talks for Preschoolers*. Cincinnati: Standard Publishing, 1996.

De Jonge, JoAnne E. *All-Occasion Object Lessons*. Grand Rapids: Baker Book House, 1996.

———. *More Object Lessons from Nature*. Grand Rapids: Baker Book House, 1991.

Draper's Book of Quotations for the Christian World. Edythe Draper, ed. Wheaton, IL: Tyndale House Publishers, 1992.

Fleming, Jean. *A Mother's Heart*. Colorado Springs: NavPress, 1987.

Gangel, Kenneth O. *Building Leaders for Church Education*. Chicago: Moody Press, 1981.

Gangel, Kenneth O. and Warren S. Benson. *Christian Education: Its History and Philosophy*. Chicago: Moody Press, 1983.

Graham, Billy. *Angels: God's Secret Agents*. Garden City, NY: Doubleday & Co., 1975.

Hendricks, Howard. *Heaven Help the Home*. Wheaton, IL: Victor Books, 1982.

Hudson, Kathi. *Raising Kids God's Way*. Wheaton, IL: Crossway Books, 1995.

Hunter, Emily. *A Child's First Steps to Virtues*. Eugene, OR: Harvest House Publishers, 1995.

Kjos, Berit. *Your Child and the New Age*. Wheaton, IL: Victor Books, 1990.

Kohr, Louise. *More In-the-Bag Stories: Object Talks for Children*. Cincinnati: Standard Publishing, 1992.

Meier, Paul D. and Linda Burnett. *A Mother's Choice*. Grand Rapids: Baker Book House, 1980.

Packer, J.I. *Knowing Christianity*. Wheaton, IL: Harold Shaw Publishers, 1995.

———. *Knowing God*. Downers Grove: InterVarsity Press, 1979.

Painter, F.V.N. *Luther on Education*. St. Louis: Concordia, 1928.

Raising them Right. Colorado Springs: Focus on the Family Publishers, 1994.

Rhodes, Ron. *Angels Among Us*. Eugene, OR: Harvest House Publishers, 1995.

———. *Heaven: The Undiscovered Country*. Eugene, OR: Harvest House Publishers, 1995.

———. *The Culting of America*. Eugene, OR: Harvest House Publishers, 1994.

———. *The Heart of Christianity*. Eugene, OR: Harvest House Publishers, 1996.

Richards, Lawrence O. *A Theology of Christian Education*. Grand Rapids: Zondervan Publishing House, 1979.

Ryrie, Charles. *You Mean the Bible Teaches That?* Chicago: Moody Press, 1978.

Schooling Choices: An Examination of Private, Public, and Home Education. H. Wayne House, ed. Portland, OR: Multnomah, 1988.

Smalley, Gary. *The Key to Your Child's Heart*. Dallas: Word Books, 1992.

Swindoll, Charles. *Growing Deep in the Christian Life*. Portland, OR: Multnomah Press, 1986.

Tan, Paul Lee. *Encyclopedia of 7,700 Illustrations*. Rockville, MD: Assurance Publishers, 1979.

Tozer, A.W. *The Knowledge of the Holy*. New York: Harper & Row, 1961.

Van Seters, Virginia Ann. *26 More Object Talks for Children's Worship*. Cincinnati: Standard Publishing, 1990.

———. *Easy Object Talks for Teaching Children*. Cincinnati: Standard Publishing, 1992.

Warren, Rick. *The Purpose-Driven Church*. Grand Rapids: Zondervan Publishing House, 1996.

What My Parents Did Right. Gloria Gaither, ed. Wheaton, IL: Tyndale House Publishers, 1991.

White, Joe. *FaithTraining*. Colorado Springs: Focus on the Family Publishers, 1994.

Zettersten, Rolf. *Train Up a Child*. Wheaton, IL: Tyndale House Publishers, 1991.